Nelson Mandela: A Very Short Introduction

VERY SHORT INTRODUCTIONS are for anyone wanting a stimulating and accessible way into a new subject. They are written by experts, and have been translated into more than 45 different languages.

The series began in 1995, and now covers a wide variety of topics in every discipline. The VSI library currently contains over 700 volumes—a Very Short Introduction to everything from Psychology and Philosophy of Science to American History and Relativity—and continues to grow in every subject area.

Very Short Introductions available now:

Available soon:

For more information visit our website

www.oup.com/vsi/

Elleke Boehmer

NELSON MANDELA

A Very Short Introduction

OXFORD
UNIVERSITY PRESS

Great Clarendon Street, Oxford, OX2 6DP,
United Kingdom

Oxford University Press is a department of the University of Oxford.
It furthers the University's objective of excellence in research, scholarship,
and education by publishing worldwide. Oxford is a registered trade mark of
Oxford University Press in the UK and in certain other countries

Published in the United States of America by Oxford University Press
198 Madison Avenue, New York, NY 10016, United States of America

British Library Cataloguing in Publication Data

Data available

Library of Congress Control Number: 2023935835

ISBN 978-0-19-289344-4

Printed and bound by
Printed by Integrated Books International, United States of America

Aan mijn familie

Contents

Acknowledgements

I have notched up a great many debts in the course of writing this *Very Short Introduction*. In roughly chronological order warm thanks go to:

Mark Allix, co-navigator through the streets of Johannesburg in the 1980s;

Rob Nixon, whose essay 'Mandela, Messianism, and the Media' opened new insights;

Robert Young, whose *Postcolonialism: VSI* set an inspiring example;

Stephen Morton and Alex Tickell, conversations with whom about colonial terror helped foster this study;

Achille Mbembe, for thoughts on violence in the postcolony;

Leela Gandhi and Catherine Clarke, for saying that a reflective postcolonial study of Mandela was long overdue;

Ed Larrissy and the School of English, University of Leeds, Simon Glendinning and the European Forum, and Mieke Bal and her ASCA team in Amsterdam, for hosting my papers on Mandela the 'postcolonial terrorist' at their conferences in 2005 and 2006;

The journal *Parallax* for publishing the article 'Postcolonial Terrorist: The Example of Nelson Mandela' in their special issue 37 on 'Agitation' (October–December 2005) that grew out of these papers;

Tim Brennan and Keya Ganguly, fellow guests at the ASCA conference, for their searching and sustaining questions;

Marsha Filion, and Luciana O'Flaherty and James Thompson at Oxford University Press, for their encouragement and help;

Derek Attridge and David Attwell, for moral support and good guidance;

Geerthi Ahilan and her 2004–5 Year 5 group at St Ebbe's C-of-E-aided Primary School, for confronting the question 'Who is Nelson Mandela?';

The Department of English at Royal Holloway, University of London, in particular the informal grant workshop group of Bob Eaglestone, Christie Carson, and Jenny Neville; also HoD Robert Hampson, fellow DoGS Ewan Fernie, Anne Varty, my commuting companion, and the irreplaceable Alice Christie—all for much appreciated help and encouragement;

The AHRC Research Leave Award AN/E503543/1 which indispensably facilitated the writing-up period;

The wonderful Royal Holloway Postcolonial Research Group for engaging with my still-unformed ideas about Mandela, in particular Helen Gilbert (for her thoughts on postcolonial performing bodies), David Lambert (for his remarkable analytic insights), Nicole King (for her deep knowledge of African American writing and politics);

Danielle Battigelli and James Rogers, for their enthusiasm and the logo-bearing apron;

Jo McDonagh, for Derrida's *Spectres* and strong cups of tea;

Susheila Nasta, my co-editor on the *Wasafiri* special 'Cultures of Terror' issue, for her insightful advice;

Shaun Johnson, CEO of the Mandela Rhodes Foundation, for indulging my speculations concerning the Madiba phenomenon;

The Department of English, University of Stellenbosch, especially Dirk Klopper and Meg Samuelson, for hosting me during a crucial period of research towards this book;

Sarah Nuttall who, rescuing me from a rainy Cape weekend, sat me down at a table spread with art books, vivid insights, and baby toys;

Isabel Hofmeyr, for her historical pointers and inspiration;

Simphiwe Yako and Andre Mohammed, archivists at the Mayibuye Archive, University of the Western Cape, and Carol Archibald of the Historical Papers Section, Cullen Library, University of the Witwatersrand, for their advice and help;

David Medalie, intrepid navigator through the streets of Johannesburg, especially Kort Street, at rush-hour, in 2006;

Karina Szczurek and Andre Brink, for their hospitality and helpful points of reference;

The Centre of Memory and Dialogue at the Nelson Mandela Foundation, especially Project Manager Verne Harris, for invaluable research support;

Mike Nicol for invigorating email chats about Madiba hagiography;

Judith Brown, for her thoughts about Gandhi the Victorian gentleman;

Josée Boehmer-Dekker, Ilona Berkhof, and the Thuiszorg team in Den Haag, for their fantastic help during my mother's final year, which was also the final year of this book's making;

Sandra Assersohn, inspired picture researcher;

Alison Donnell, Saul Dubow, and Steven Matthews, for thoughtful readings of the final manuscript at a busy time, and William Beinart for his attuned and measured commentary;

Steven Matthews, again, and Thomas and Sam Matthews Boehmer, for keeping the world turning, and the sun spinning through the sky.

In preparing the second edition of this *Very Short Introduction*, in 2020–2, I have had further enriching conversations on Mandela with a number of generous people. In particular I should like to thank: Rita Barnard; William Beinart (again) and Colin Bundy, editors of *Reassessing Mandela* (2020); Shireen Hassim, Thula Simpson, Tom Lodge, and the other contributors to *Reassessing Mandela*; Edward Brookes and Michael Lamb, for their reflections on 21st-century leadership; Jonny Steinberg, for an inspiring and helpful conversation about the Mandelas in 2021; and my remarkable interlocutors on the *Mandela Rhodes Story* project, Abigail McDougall, Mako Muzenda, and Iris Nxumalo-De Smidt. I continued to learn from Shaun Johnson's insights and collaboration with Mandela when working on both this second edition, and the *Mandela Rhodes Story* manuscript, co-authored with him. Research assistance from the astute and indefatigable Bhagya Casaba Somashekar has been invaluable throughout.

Kind acknowledgement to Faber and Faber Ltd for permission to quote 'Brief Dream' from *Collected Poems* by Samuel Beckett (2007). The poem first appeared in Jacques Derrida and Mustafa Tlili (eds), *For Nelson Mandela* (Seaver Books, 1986). I am also grateful to Koleka Putuma and Manyano Media Management for permission to quote from '1994: a love poem', from the collection *Collective Amnesia* (uHlanga Press, 2017).

List of illustrations

The publisher and the author apologize for any errors or omissions in the above list. If contacted they will be pleased to rectify these at the earliest opportunity.

List of abbreviations

AAM	Anti-Apartheid Movement
ANC	African National Congress
ANCYL	African National Congress Youth League
ARM	African Resistance Movement
BCM	Black Consciousness Movement
CODESA	Convention for a Democratic South Africa
GEAR	Growth, Employment, and Redistribution (modification of South Africa's Reconstruction and Development Programme)
GNU	Government of National Unity
MK	Umkhonto we Sizwe ('Spear of the Nation')
OAU	Organisation of African Unity
PAC	Pan-Africanist Congress
PAFMECA	Pan-African Freedom Movement for East and Central Africa
SACP	South African Communist Party
SAIC	South African Indian Congress
SASOL	South African Coal, Oil and Gas Corporation
SRC	Students' Representative Council
SWAPO	South-West Africa People's Organisation
TRC	Truth and Reconciliation Commission
UDF	United Democratic Front

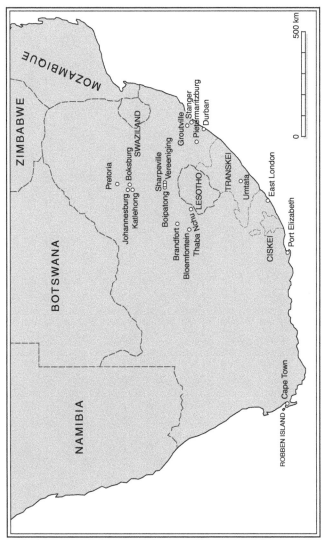

Map of South Africa during apartheid.

Chapter 1
Mandela: Story and symbol

His given Xhosa name *Rolihlahla* signified he could be a troublemaker. His clan honorific *Madiba* associated him with his aristocratic Thembu lineage. And his European name *Nelson*, his best-known name, given to him by his primary school teacher, imprinted his life with the name of one of imperial Britain's naval heroes. Between these three nodal points of his names—signifying resistance, social stature, and heroism, respectively—Nelson Rolihlahla Mandela's life played out in extraordinary, myth-making ways. By the 20th-century's end, his face and his form, his raised-arm salute and walk into freedom, were among its widely reproduced political icons. A decade and more after his death in 2013, Mandela remains one of the best-known leaders of the Global South; probably still one of the most highly regarded politicians the postcolonial world has known. In South Africa, however, his reputation in some circles is reduced and he is perceived to have presided over an incomplete political transformation. Elsewhere, he is still seen as a transformative figure without whom reconciliation in his country could not have been achieved.

Nelson Mandela—is it possible to say, in a phrase, who or what he was? And what he stood for? Yes, he was one of the world's longest detained political prisoners and, during the time of his incarceration, easily its most famous. He is a universal symbol of social justice certainly, an exemplary figure connoting non-racialism and democracy, a moral giant. Once a man without a face (photographs of political prisoners in South Africa being banned), he became after his 1990 release an internationally recognizable image. For over four decades, while his country was vilified the world over for its policies of state-sanctioned racism of apartheid, Mandela symbolically, and to some extent practically, led the movement of resistance to that injustice. Even when subsequent misgovernment and ongoing racial division called South Africa's reconciliation experiment into serious question, he continues to stand as a beacon of anti-racial struggle.

Why should Mandela's story be important to us in the world at large? What do his achievements signify, not only nationally in South Africa but also internationally? How is it that he also became a big name worldwide—a prominent figure in the campaign to raise HIV/AIDS awareness; the 2006 Amnesty International ambassador of conscience; a moniker in UK comedy shows (Mark Thomas's *As Used on the Famous Nelson Mandela)?* Why is his face still chosen to grace the covers of potted histories of our time alongside, say, human rights activist Malala Yousafzai or the environmentalist Greta Thunberg? How was it that at the time of the unveiling of his statue in Westminster Square in the summer of 2007, he was hailed as 'President of the World' (by analogy with the 'People's Princess' Diana)?

> If one wanted an example of an absolutely upright man, that man, that example would be Mandela. If one wanted an example of an unshakably firm, courageous, heroic, calm, intelligent, and capable man, that example and that man would be Mandela...I identify him as one of the most extraordinary symbols of this era.
>
> Fidel Castro, from 'We Will Never Return to the Slave Barracks' (1991)

In the celebrity culture that marks the 21st century, with its focus on the individual as maker of their destiny, it is often assumed

Nelson Mandela

that Mandela was not only the master of his individual fate (as his favourite poem puts it), but the chief architect of the new South Africa. It is taken as read that he fought a single-handed fight for the rights of black people, and that in his case the theory that Great Men make history is well justified. And yet, as he himself often reminded people, his nation South Africa's liberation struggle was effectively fought for and won while he languished in gaol. Already at his 1962 trial he emphasized, 'I have been only one in a large army of people'.

After his release from political imprisonment, his personal charisma quickly became famous. All who met him remarked on the palpable charm, the *Madiba magic*, that radiated from him: a combination of his fame, height, and good looks, his encyclopaedic memory for faces, his can-do qualities, plus an indefinable something else, an attractive Mandela-esque *je ne sais quoi*. Central to his character, wrote his admirer the novelist Nadine Gordimer, is 'a remove from self-centredness, the capacity to live for others'. His good guidance and charisma represented important sources of inspiration for the making of post-1994 South Africa. It is also true that he did not himself, strictly speaking, author that new democracy. With Mandela it is manifestly the case that his leadership *alone* cannot explain the historical development in South Africa from apartheid to freedom. Inner radiance alone cannot account for why his icon should continue to bulk large both nationally and internationally.

The true picture—the real-life constituents of Madiba magic—is a great deal more complicated than the story of individual specialness suggests. It is based in a quality of character certainly, but this is combined with other key factors which this book addresses, not least his talent as a performer, and career-long proximity to several outstanding colleagues and friends, themselves astute political minds, especially Oliver Tambo, Walter Sisulu, and Ahmed Kathrada. Then there are the ways in which his social make-up impacted on political developments in his country, especially in the 1950s, and how he shaped and reshaped his nationalist stance in response to those developments, while also increasingly reaching for transnational models of resistance, and appealing to an international audience. Throughout, he both referenced and drew upon, yet worked in skilful counterpoint to, his highborn background and its legacies of consensual authority, in order to shape the democratic, collective leadership structures of his organization, the African National Congress (ANC).

> Let us not make Nelson Mandela some kind of icon on a pedestal belonging to a museum. He is a wave in an ocean, part of a rich tradition that raises certain kinds of questions, beginning with our own lives and our willingness to muster the courage to examine who we are as humans.
>
> Cornel West, 'Nelson Mandela' (2007)

A mundane point to make about a memorable man it may be, yet Nelson Mandela is one of those historical figures who, in the mid- to late 1950s, and then in the 1980s and 1990s, was not merely the right man to stand forth at the right time. He was also, importantly, the one who did so with notable political acumen, adaptability, and style, as well as self-consciously and determinedly, and, as Cornel West writes, with 'a certain Socratic fire'. At a time when the polarized racial struggle in South Africa justified a sharp turn from till-then effective passive resistance to a more militant response, he spearheaded the difficult decision to take up arms, and was able to persuade his organization to support the new line of action. But when, thirty years on, he deemed that the time had come to move beyond warring polarities towards the negotiation table, again he found the means to stand upon his moral status, push through that decision, and take his organization with him. Repeatedly, he created a role for himself within the ANC's structure and ideological landscape, and then exceeded it. Never doubting he had right on his side, he retained faith in his vision of a non-discriminatory South Africa through

4

twenty-seven years of incarceration. Eventually, he staked a place in his nation's future, as a figure embodying not only justice, but also, above all, hope.

Nelson Mandela: The story

This book is about the different, interconnected stories, histories, symbols, and values that are referred to using the 'famous' name *Nelson Mandela*. As captured in the Zapiro cartoon marking his 80th birthday (Figure 1), across his life Mandela filled a rich range of roles: diligent student, city-slicker, dashing guerrilla, the world's longest suffering political prisoner, the millennial saviour figure. He proved to be a versatile, even postmodern, shape-shifter who at each stage of his career, or his shape-shifting, succeeded in projecting an omnibus appeal. A variety of different constituencies—black nationalists and white communists, rugby players and novelists, world leaders and township dwellers—feeling themselves addressed by him, claimed his emblem for themselves.

1. Destined to play a bewildering array of roles.

Mandela the tale represents individual journeying and overcoming, but it also *at the same time* tells the collective, many-voiced story of a nation's coming-into-being.

One of the prominent stories associated with the name Nelson Mandela is inevitably a nationalist story, a *nation's story*. From around the midpoint of his presidency, 1997, Mandela's life narrative was officially elevated as South Africa's main governing tale, its modern myth, as reflected in government school-reader and children's cartoon-book histories. His autobiography *Long Walk to Freedom* (1994) was often styled as a parable in democracy building. In his biographies, the character and thought of the historical figure are everywhere overlaid with faithful accounts of the political-historical processes in which he was involved. At a more general level, as if to reinforce these representations of the national saviour, condensed histories of the 20th century enshrine the Mandela story as one of the few ethically affirming national tales to emerge from its decades of devastating conflict, often between rival nations.

A short introduction to the career of a figure bulging with this kind of national meaning—not to say heroic symbolization—presents obvious pitfalls, not least the temptation to reproduce the dominant accounts of the secular saint and architect of democracy, where surprisingly few other interpretations exist. The more scholarly biographical studies of Mandela (by Benson, Meer, Sampson, Meredith, Lodge, Mangcu, and Bundy, among others) tend to approach him by his own lights, as, for example, the determined leader of the more militant tendency in the ANC, or as the disciplined pilot of his country's destiny. Writing at different historical moments, as new archival sources incrementally open up, the biographers differ in their interpretations of his political role, yet they do not take issue with his national symbolic significance. For each and every one, Mandela embodies a post-apartheid South Africa. For some, additionally, he remains a model, a history with a nationalist moral attached, a pedagogic tale bearing political truth.

For Benson in 1986, writing at the quarter-century point of his incarceration, Mandela is all liberal democrat and responsible party man, a reassuring figure for sceptical western audiences (and noticeably less radical than in a 1965 collection of articles edited by communist colleague Ruth First). For Meer in 1988, prior to the uncertain hour of his release, he is the consummate patrician, translating familial and ethnic loyalties into a strong network of nationalist affiliation. For Sampson, author of still the most authoritative biography to date, Mandela is in 1999, at the end of his presidency, a shining example of unifying leadership, at once western and African, 'the people's president'. For the political historian Lodge, in a cooler though still admiring portrait, Mandela accommodates his charismatic authority to protect South Africa's fragile structures of democratic politics. For Xolela Mangcu, he gives world history an African and a human face.

Despite their varying assessments of his politics, each individual historian clearly takes the decision to cooperate with a dominant strain in Mandela's own make-up: his emphasis on how a leader's work for the nation moulds his own future, and vice versa. This emphasis is reflected, too, in the numerous African leaders' (auto) biographies published since 1950—by Nkrumah, Azikiwe, Kaunda, amongst others—to mark the moment of their country's independence, to which group Mandela's obviously belongs. Typically, in most of these biographical narratives, the upward trajectory of the life is amplified by way of a process of metaphorical extension, whereby the story is projected through the exemplary patterns of pilgrimage and metamorphosis. The biographical subject's long period of removal from the world, in gaol or in exile, for example, is often followed in the biography by miraculous change or transformation, intended as edifying for readers.

Over-determined though he may be as the symbol of democratic South Africa, this book cannot sidestep telling the iconic national story that the name Nelson Mandela denotes. That story was confirmed and illuminated by the thousands of candle-lit shrines that emerged on street corners after his death on 6 December 2013, and his state funeral and burial at Qunu, Transkei on 15 December. His achievement is probably incomprehensible outside the historical context of South Africa's freedom struggle, which he did choreograph in several ways. 'Mandela's story is central to an understanding of the outcome of the liberation struggle', cultural historian Annie Coombs writes. In other words, this book approaches the national Mandela story conventionally, which is to say chronologically, across two chapters of scene-setting, from a narrative viewpoint which almost inevitably assumes the metaphorical sub-structure of the long walk and the slow, upward climb. Though I retrace certain familiar pathways, reinforced by a supporting timeline of important dates and events, this book attempts, however, to refrain from enshrining Mandela as exemplary. Cross-sectional digressions and sideways pointers to other possible readings will fret the smooth progression of the biographical narrative, anticipating the five topic-based chapters that follow.

Bearing in mind how Mandela worked throughout as the astute author of his own image, these later chapters set out to offer a more interpretative account of the defining episodes of his biography and key aspects of his approach and achievement. Though sometimes sidelined in the biographical studies, these aspects are arguably as important as his national vision in bulwarking his international stature. The alternative windows on Mandela focus, *inter alia*, on his cosmopolitan receptivity to transnational political influences; his protean skills as an urban performer yet projector of an uncompromising masculinity; his 'dialogic' prison garden projects; and his international repute as the humanist 'icon who outgrew his country' (journalist Shaun Johnson's phrase). In this way, the study in its latter half offers a more interiorized, speculative analysis of Mandela than biographies centred on the towering public figure as a rule provide—one that, in the first edition of this book, proved influential in laying the ground for the more thematic approach to Mandela's life that other studies have since helped to trace.

The book's approach via a range of themed (though still chronologically based) readings is informed by anthropologist James Clifford's fruitful idea that an individual life constitutes 'a narrative of trans-individual occasions', a crossing point between different inspirations, motivations, traditions, relationships, and roles. The accent will be on how individual histories are formed in relation to one another, in connection with struggles and counter-struggles in other places. True, the crosshatched or synchronic perspective may initially seem counter-intuitive, given the apparent coherence of the messianic Mandela figure in media and government representations. On reflection, however, it is evident not only that Mandela's life was always remarkably networked, a busy meeting place of different ideologies and influences (at a time before the 24/7 media access that today's politicians take for granted). It is also true that, as a consummate performer, he often chose to operate in several different registers, deploying various personae, either simultaneously or sequentially.

Although Mandela till 1990 led a necessarily nation-bound, or indeed island-bound, existence, from the time of his arrival in Johannesburg as a young man in the 1940s, his political project and resistance theory were consistently formed in discussion with colleagues and rivals. Not by nature a contemplative figure, it was these networks that made of him, first, an influential political activist, and later, with the long incarceration, a thoughtful negotiator. Moreover, to the same degree as his life was not confined to a single, nationalist track, so too did his career not fall into discrete phases. There were preoccupations, interests, and responses that either ran across the life or, alternatively, looped back, connecting with earlier phases. The Sophiatown sophisticate of the 1950s returned in the 1990s figure of the debonair statesman. The mission-school student found a new incarnation in the self-disciplined Robben Island letter-writer. Far from being limited to a one-directional pathway to freedom, the story of his life crystallizes into clusters of encounters, practices, possibilities, and agendas.

In short, rather than admiring Mandela as such, this book considers the *processes of meaning-making* (including his own) which have caused his achievement to be admired. As a function of its different readings, the discussion will acknowledge that Mandela was in some ways an unlikely figure to have received the kind of adulation that was showered upon him. It is difficult to think of a more outstanding international figure who was so long out of the public eye, whose major speeches were so often formulaic and rhetorically cautious, and whose many sacrifices in the cause of non-racialism are now at times called into question as inadequate.

Reading Madiba

To calibrate his unidirectional national story against his diverse other preoccupations, it is important to pose at this point the specific question of which readings of Mandela present themselves as alternatives to the national myth. What are the other interpretative approaches that cast light on the governing preoccupations of his life? How might we encapsulate the 'takes' on the first democratic South African president that draw out his different domains of involvement and appeal?

To begin with, alongside the straightforward Mandela-as-new-South-Africa reading, in which he is the chief protagonist within a national drama, there is a *global story* featuring Mandela. Beginning in the 1960s, when his court addresses first drew the world's attention, and resuming in 1988 with his televised 70th 'birthday party' at Wembley, he became in the eyes of others the definition of a world icon. In the media he was constructed, even produced, as a pre-eminent symbol within an ongoing struggle against exploitation not confined to South Africa. In the 2000s it was claimed that Mandela was second only to Coca-Cola as the world's most recognizable name. Even if this was only partly true, it certainly is the case that his image appears to resonate with values important to a global community once interconnected by its opposition to apartheid—values including courage, perseverance, and justice. In a world where Cold War certainties had collapsed, Mandela stood for many as a beacon of new humanism and hope for change. In this capacity, Nadine Gordimer observed, he 'belongs to the world'. Several chapters will touch on the global dimensions of Mandela's ethical-political legacy.

Mandela's story is also crucially, even quintessentially, the story of an African *quest for modernity*. Here modernity should not be understood as equivalent to colonialism, but as involving a claim to selfhood, to being a subject of history, that is expressed through a process of transposing the vocabularies of modern identity into African contexts. Where colonialism impacts on this story is in so far as African subjectivity was routinely excluded from official accounts of European historical progress: in colonial discourse Africa tended to signify emptiness, a heart of darkness, or mere physicality.

By contrast, any study of Mandela charts a decades-long narrative of black South African political leadership-in-the-making; of how, in a situation of extreme racial discrimination, African individuals and communities set about claiming self-determination, citizenship, and democratic rights. From the time that Mandela the country youth arrived in the city of Johannesburg to find work, he formed a central part of an educated elite that insisted on the right to belong there (as against being confined to the rural hinterland) and sought to accommodate itself within its public spaces. As Chapters 5 and 6 on Mandela as urban dweller and performer suggest, he boldly created a malleable modern identity by engaging with the city's heterogeneous cultural and political resources. As for his literary counterparts, the writers and journalists of Sophiatown, his legal work, newspaper articles, and speeches translated modernity into local terms, to forge the conditions for the emergence of a black South African citizenry.

In effect, Mandela's story tracks the complicated, inventive ways in which modern life was moulded in decolonizing Africa. The uneven introduction of European modernity, whether in rural communities or the Johannesburg townships, encouraged the black elite creatively to deploy different social roles and languages at once to question colonial stereotypes *and* assert themselves as transformative agents within their communities. In South Africa, as in other once-colonized places, projecting oneself as a contemporary individual involved a continual shuttling between different frames of cultural reference, a running together of discrepant though temporally coincident interpretations of one's place in history, as Dipesh Chakrabarty describes.

The narrative of Mandela's quest for modernity represents a powerful way of accounting for the layeredness of his life-story, for how he managed to assume different, seemingly contradictory positions. At times, he crossed a reconstituted concept of Thembu political tradition with the conventions of modern western democracy; at others he pitted the aggressive, go-getting energies of urban modernity against the primitivist stereotypes that were favoured under apartheid. Indeed, Mandela's quest-story carries a particular late-20th-century irony. In his case, far from being seen as a belated African addition to the history of modern self-making, he is now regarded by many, even if in an over-compensatory way, as himself a maker of modern history, as occupying a highpoint in the global struggle for self-determination and human rights.

Seeing Mandela as the choreographer of an adaptive, capacious African modernity correlates with a related reading: one that views many aspects of his political achievement, first as a militant and then as a negotiator, as definitively *postcolonial*. Mandela's energies were always devoted to restoring black South Africans to their buried histories of resistance, to overcoming colonial legacies of power by taking over the languages and the laws of that power to effect that overcoming. Both are essentially postcolonial undertakings. As Phil Bonner also writes, though Mandela was a politician first and foremost, rather than an intellectual or thinker, his work (political activism, critical writings, and speeches) presents us with an intensely *practical* discourse of anti-colonial resistance: that is to say, with an anti- or postcolonial *theory-in-practice*. His achievement lay in demonstrating how an oppressive situation could be withstood through a process of strategically repeating and exceeding the oppressor's self-justifying discourses of rationality or belonging. As Chapters 7 and 8 explore, Mandela generated late humanist concepts of resistance and reconciliation through his lifelong, always intensely dialogic, political dealings. Though in the 2010s his transformative impact as a politician was called into question, this book contends that his work against apartheid nonetheless represented a serious-minded anti-colonial and human rights struggle.

His release from prison projected an unchallenged, patriarchal voice, a voice rooted in the most intense physical conflict between blacks and whites on this planet, the final frontier of white supremacy on the African continent, out across the relay systems of the black Atlantic.

Paul Gilroy, from *The Black Atlantic* (1993)

Across the decolonizing decades of the 20th century, postcolonial thought found its stimulus and structure in anti-colonial practice, as theorists like Benita Parry and Robert Young explain. This book extends the territory of this criticism. It makes the case that by helping to bring into being the new democratic South Africa,

Nelson Mandela effectively became a postcolonial theorist-of-a-kind.

True, Mandela's political and ethical achievements are not widely recognized as theoretically significant, for at least two reasons. First, in so far as he was, controversially, an advocate of militant resistance for some part of his career, he was preceded in his arguments for armed struggle both by his Communist Party comrades and by the prominent theorist Frantz Fanon. As Chapter 4 on Mandela's influences suggests, Fanon's powerful justification of anti-colonial violence is likely to have had a shaping effect on the ANC's shift to armed resistance in 1961. Mandela was no flag-bearer in this respect. Second, the relative theoretical invisibility of Mandela is in part also because, unlike M. K. Gandhi, he was never as resistant as was the Indian leader to articulating his opposition to the repressive state in the self-same cultural terms as deployed by that state. He invoked the priority of Europe (if selectively), including its notions of modern progress and 'civilized' values, in order to frame his critique of apartheid.

This book's postcolonial reading of Mandela, which runs across its second half, will allow us to gain critical purchase precisely on contradictory articulations such as these. If postcolonialism is defined as the attempt by the world's marginalized to lay claim to its centres of meaning, then Mandela's efforts to promote African cultural values and indigenous histories of freedom struggle are unequivocally postcolonial, even, arguably, decolonial. Yet so, too, was his pragmatic empathy for the rival nationalist position of South Africa's Afrikaner minority in the 1980s—an identification that pushed him towards the risky bid for cross-racial conciliation. For him, intrinsically African qualities of reciprocal brotherhood and consensualism were, at the same time, intensely human qualities: *Africanness* and *humanness* were radically co-extensive, not oppositional.

The ubiquitous icon of an era

The long road to freedom is a never-ending road: with this widely cited image Mandela ends his autobiography. His life, unfolding in proximity to a lively black literary culture, spawned many enduring metaphors. Regent's ward, Black Pimpernel, prison-cell scholar, master of fate, life-long pilgrim towards democracy: throughout Mandela was perceived, and perceived himself, in strongly symbolic and mythic terms, to an extent that justifies a *literary reading* of his achievement. Indeed, it is safe to say that Mandela has so consistently lived in ways governed by form-giving images and generic patterns that his life has been itself built into metaphor, as several poems and novels record. If across the 1970s and 1980s apartheid was internationally seen as a timeless referent of iniquity, then the figure who led the struggle against that iniquity, ironically, absorbed something of that iconic timelessness.

Sections of the themed chapters that follow, especially Chapters 6 and 7, consider the many figurative aspects of *Mandela*, the story and the icon. Weighing the many historical and biographical interpretations that have appeared, they offer reflections on the powerful tendency towards self-symbolization and performance that marked his adult experience. From the time he became a successful lawyer, then a charismatic nationalist, Mandela set himself up as the realization of his people's expectations. Throughout, he remained acutely aware that power requires symbolism and myth for its elevation, to the extent that he became himself a totem of turn-of-the-century totemic values—toleration and liberal democracy.

In the years following his death, Mandela's halo lost some of its lustre, with the tarnishing of the ANC's reputation during the corrupt Jacob Zuma presidency (2009–18), and the so-called Fallist movements of the 2010s, as explored in Chapter 8.

Some young South Africans, sometimes called Afro-pessimists, now question Mandela's emphasis on racial reconciliation over economic restructuring. However, even this changed view of Mandela is understood in terms of media image, national metaphor, and moral example. In the 2020s, Nelson Mandela remains one of the most prominent political celebrities to hail from the Global South. For many, he still stands as a towering global hero and, even in his own still-divided country, not only a warrior against racial injustice, but as a bold and creative artist of social change built through human understanding.

Chapter 2
Scripting a life: The early years

Any attempt to narrate the life of Nelson Mandela confronts the difficulty that to do so is to tell a double-framed story—of South Africa, and of Mandela-in-South-Africa, in the second half of the 20th century and into the 21st. As the title of his 1978 collection of speeches *The Struggle Is My Life* announces, from the time of the 1952 Defiance Campaign, Mandela's actions were intensively informed by—interactive with and against—the operations of the South African state. This was publicly so until 1964; then again, decisively, from 1990; and covertly in the intervening years.

Indeed, as is often the case in nations undergoing regeneration after periods of trouble, the biography of Mandela the First President was, especially at the highpoint of his reputation, often held up as the definitive history of the new South Africa's coming-into-being. Moreover, to the degree to which that national story is now seen as incomplete, Mandela's reputation, too, has been impacted by association. For modern nationalism it is generally true to say that a nation is understood by both its citizens and the international community through the medium of a rallying symbolic tale recounting how it was constituted. In South Africa that pre-eminent story is still Nelson's story. As for other national heroes—Bolivar, Napoleon, Nehru—Mandela's life-story and character are seen as beacons of national achievement.

Worshipful nationalist biography or hagiography is perhaps especially acute when the nation, as in the case of South Africa, has been born, or in fact twice-born, out of racial conflict and repression. The 1910 Union of South Africa was forged on the basis of a fragile unity of Afrikaners and English-speaking white people after the Anglo-Boer War (1899–1902)—the culmination of a series of wars over land and resources fought between British and Dutch settlers and indigenous black populations across the 19th century. The unified settler colony's underlying geography and overarching state structures were from the start strongly racialized, and in subsequent decades the Afrikaners' sense of marginalization by British-descended settlers only fuelled their already defensive nationalism. In 1948 the reformed Afrikaner Nationalist Party won victory on the ticket of founding a white-dominated state. As Mandela would himself recognize, the history of 20th-century South Africa was profoundly shaped by the fierce contest between two nationalisms, Afrikaner and African, for the 'same piece of earth'.

A second, related yet separate, difficulty with recounting Mandela's life concerns the generic, especially allegorical, patterns through which his story tends to be narrated. In all of the biographies bar none, the authors of Mandela the Life assume a more or less onward-and-upward trajectory, fitting the overarching motif of a journey or pilgrimage signalled in his autobiography's title. This suggests that the 'long walk to freedom' may be tough and uphill but it begins with a rural idyll, proceeds through setbacks and difficulties, and ends, as does that of Christian in Bunyan's *The Pilgrim's Progress* (1678), with the achievement of the Celestial City, the free, democratic nation. The steady-climb metaphor subtends the number of beginner's guides widely available in South Africa and beyond, including the soft-focus *Madiba* by Lionel Maxim, the 'They Fought for Freedom' and 'Famous Lives' series contributions, and the Nelson Mandela Foundation's own 'Madiba Legacy' comic-book series. But the standard biographies, too—Meer's, Sampson's,

Meredith's—at times intermittently, yet also unmistakably, adopt the ready-made journey motif. Even Colin Bundy's 'post-hagiographic' Jacana pocket biography (2015) reads Mandela's life in terms of his career trajectory and the process of myth-building that informed it.

The ubiquity of the life-journey trope in Nelson's story pertains not only to the aura that accrued over the prison years to *No Easy Walk to Freedom:* the Nehru-inspired title of his 1965 collection of speeches which was confirmed in the title of his later autobiography. It also attaches closely to the prevalence of ideas of redemptive onward journeying in African writing generally, which links with the influential role played by Bunyan's *The Pilgrim's Progress* in the mission-school education of many mid-20th-century African writers, intellectuals, and politicians, as Isabel Hofmeyr's *The Portable Bunyan* explains. Christian's story appealed powerfully to young African readers fortified by the values of community and hard work inculcated through their rural, traditional, often Christianized childhoods, even as they battled to forge self-reliance in a context hostile to black opportunity. The journey framework offered African writers a symbolic space within which to plot patterns of incremental self-improvement and progress (whether towards modernity or back to tradition). Any number of autobiographical African *Bildungsromane* appearing from the 1940s onwards follow the same trajectory: Camara Laye's *L'Enfant noir* (1954), Mphahlele's *Down Second Avenue* (1959), Achebe's *No Longer at Ease* (1960), Ngugi's *Weep Not, Child* (1964).

Mandela's story exhibits, too, a recognizable typicality and representativeness, underpinned by a teleology of political growth with liberation as its goal. By recounting a steady progression towards freedom and modernity, despite inevitable setbacks, the life-story runs in parallel with the largely masculine, one-directional narrative of resistance and overcoming as it has been played out in Africa and elsewhere in the once-colonized world. As such, his tale shares common ground with the biographies and memoirs, too, of his colleagues Walter Sisulu, Oliver Tambo, and Albert Luthuli. Beginning with the ANC's regeneration through the Youth League in the 1940s, the iconic Mandela life-story traces a path through the 'festive activism' of the 1950s, the 1960s years of incarceration and exile, the resurgent militancy of the post-1976 period, the 1990s' slow strategizing, achievement of liberation, and first presidency, and the 2000s period of 'retirement from retirement'. The youth raised in a high-status Thembu household becomes the pioneering black lawyer and political leader who finally emerges, after twenty-seven desert years, as the new South Africa's first democratic president. The enmeshing of the models of upward mobility with motifs of travel and pilgrimage is further emphasized in Mandela's autobiography by the important role played there by transformative journeys. On the first drive to school in Jongintaba's Ford, on the long car ride to Johannesburg, city of electric light, on his 1962 trip around Africa, Nelson the protagonist of the tale repeatedly has his aspirations encouraged and reconfirmed. The journey conforms to a trope of progress, driven, as is Christian of *The Pilgrim's Progress*, by 'dedicated and principled effort'. Throughout, Mandela's vision of life was of an uphill path climbed by dint of discipline and hard work.

> With the mutilation and decline of the conquered tribe a new shaman or artist struggles to emerge who finds himself moving along the knife-edge of change. He has been, as it were, cross-fertilized by victor and victim and a powerful need arises to invoke the lost generations, in a new, creative, visionary light. It is a task which is profoundly personal (and archetypal) and, therefore, accompanying an enormous potency for change—for vision into resources—runs the danger of self-enactment or hubris.
>
> Wilson Harris, from *Explorations* (1981)

This book's two different approaches, the one founded on the teleological pathway, the other topic-based and focused on the diffuse processes shaping a life, operate in contrastive ways, though always in relation to one another. The cross-section studies in the key phases of his subjectivity—examining his 'Gandhian' make-up or cosmopolitan selfhood—can best be appreciated in their complexity when mapped against the life narrative covered in this and the next chapter, with the watershed moment of incarceration serving as the dividing line between them.

The young Mandela

Rolihlahla Mandela was born on 18 July 1918 in the hamlet of Mvezo in the Transkei, the eastern region of the present-day Eastern Cape province, a rolling landscape of great loveliness after rain, and of intense poverty. It was in this land that Mandela later chose to be buried. The Transkei, once the terrain of the widely dispersed isiXhosa-speaking peoples, comprising twelve chieftaincies including the abaThembu, was at the time a peasant reserve, the largest area in South Africa where, under the 1913 Land Act restrictions, Africans could still collectively own land. Though the Thembu royalty had generally steered clear of involvement in the vicious 19th-century Frontier or Xhosa Wars (and at times sided with the British), Mandela as a youth would have witnessed how society around him remained scarred by the painful legacy of these conflicts. Sparked by British colonial encroachment onto Xhosa lands from the 1770s, the Frontier Wars had left the people divided and dispossessed, smarting at their loss of independence. The Xhosa mourned, too, the loss of their livestock following the mass panic of the 1856–7 Cattle Killings (though the Thembu again were left relatively unscathed). Much later on, between 1976 and 1994, Transkei held the dubious status of being the apartheid state's first notionally independent black homeland under Mandela's relative, Chief Kaiser Matanzima.

Mandela was born into a high-ranking family of the Xhosa-speaking Thembu chieftaincy. This made him keenly aware from childhood of the stain to ancestral honour—yet proud legacy of resistance and self-reliance—that the Frontier conflicts with the British represented, as the preambles to his 1962 and 1964 addresses to the court both emphasize. In his childhood and youth, he was at key points reminded of the lost glories of the African past, especially of the Xhosa-speaking nations. He remembered Chief Joyi, a prominent elder, railing against white injustice in his guardian's courtyard. At his circumcision, Chief Meligqili spoke a litany for the dying flower of the Xhosa peoples, 'slaves in our own land'. And when the Xhosa poet S. E. Krune Mqhayi paid a visit to Mandela's school Healdtown wearing traditional dress, he recited one of his dramatic poems based on *isibongi* (praise-songs) in which he bestirred the students to cast off 'foreign notions'.

Rolihlahla's mother, Nonqaphi Nosekeni (Fanny after her conversion to Methodism at Qunu), was the third wife of four of Gadla Henry Mpakhanyiswa, the tall, stern headman of the Mvezo area, advisor to Thembuland's Paramount Chief David Dalindyebo. A descendant of a minor house (Ixhiba) of the royal lineage of the Thembus, within a polygamous system in which birth order translated into status, Gadla did not hold the highest office, but he did serve as councillor on the Transkei Bhunga, as Xolela Mangcu emphasizes. Mandela, too, though his father's fourth son, seems to have been preferred due to his mother's favoured status. His sense of entitlement as a royal, though a minor one, and as his mother's first-born (followed by three sisters), early on bequeathed to him the conviction that he, too, was headed for the role of chief's advisor. This profound sense that 'roots were...destiny' remained with him for many years before he was able to objectify and view it more critically.

When the young Mandela was around 2 years old, a local white magistrate charged Gadla Henry with insubordination. Already at this point a white grid of authority tightly enmeshed the indigenous structures of Transkei power. Gadla was dismissed as headman and, losing income as well as status, was forced to move Nosekeni's branch of the family to Qunu village, located on the motorway from Durban to Cape Town, where Mandela's grave now lies.

At Qunu, the young Mandela was singled out by the influential, westernized Mbekela brothers as a bright child with good prospects. He was baptized a Methodist and, aged 8, sent to the village school. He attended wearing a cut-off pair of his father's trousers, his first garment of this kind, and experienced all at once the aura that comes with wearing the right costume: 'being dressed properly'. This was later confirmed in his favourite household task of pressing his guardian's suits. Although at this point he spoke no English, his teacher Miss Mdingane gave him his for-white-people-pronounceable 'English' name, Nelson. A Christian name was a customary tag for Africans in colonial society, and served as a marker of their belief. Outside the classroom he enjoyed a carefree pastoral childhood of herding, outdoor games, and fireside tales. In these years he gained an appreciation of the open veld, 'the simple beauty of nature, and the pure line of the horizon', images that would sustain him in prison. These words, written in a letter to his friend Frieda Matthews, surface in almost the same form in his autobiography.

In 1927, Mandela's father died of a lung disease, probably tuberculosis. He had, not long before, entrusted his promising youngest son to the Thembu regent Jongintaba Dalindyebo's house to be further educated and 'prepared for a wide world'. Feeling 'cut adrift', at once awestruck and bewildered, Mandela carrying a tin trunk accompanied his mother to Mqhekezweni, Jongintaba's impressive 'Great Place', a large compound comprising African huts and western-style houses. Here she handed him over to the care of the man who would from then on, for over a decade, act as his guardian and the shaper of his aspirations. Thereafter, her son would see her only infrequently, something that Mandela later regretted and mourned.

The boy Nelson quickly developed a close bond with his guardian's extrovert, slightly older son, Justice Bambilanga, and joined in with his many activities—churchgoing, ballroom dancing, and reading the *Chambers English Reader* at school. Yet, despite the stimulation that this 'sophisticated', prosperous new homestead with its wooden floorboards and Jongintaba's 'majestic' Ford V8 car offered, Nelson would always experience a keen sense of abandonment. In social contexts, this translated into an air of lofty distance, a shield against expressing grief. He had within only a few weeks lost his two closest family ties, his mother and his father, and though he was known during these years as a prankster, some of the teases involved petty theft (corn, pigs, cattle) and bed-hopping forced by bed-wetting, which suggests a certain level of insecurity. He fitted the mould of a late developer—serious, uncertain, mindful to a fault of his mentor's injunctions. Surely yet quite slowly, he developed confidence at school.

Among his most formative experiences at the Great Place was the opportunity he had to observe customary consensual democracy at work, in the form of Jongintaba's on-the-job chieftaincy. Nelson watched how the all-male, open-air tribal meetings were conducted: the enactment of fellowship through discussion; Jongintaba's attentive listening to the chiefs' cases; his attempts at the end of the meeting to forge unanimity. This spectacle of working towards consensus had, according to *Long Walk to Freedom*, a shaping effect on Mandela's later style of leadership. At this stage, we remember, Mandela had as yet had little or no contact with the world of white authority whereas, by contrast, the manner in which his guardian disposed of his power had till now entirely determined his view of the world.

Any retrospective construction, as in *Long Walk to Freedom* and the biographies based on it, is subject to a certain amount of allegorical inflation, especially during periods like the 1990s, when the ideal of African social harmony carried special symbolic resonance. It is evident that Mandela's respect for liberal or what he called 'ordinary' democracy was at many points in his career equally as strong as, if not stronger than, his allegiance to consensual decision-making, and his susceptibility to the mythic imagery of pre-colonial village democracy. However, the autobiographical account makes clear that the longwinded yet wisely managed meetings in the chief's courtyard represented an important lesson for the young Mandela in how agreement between competing views might be achieved: how patrimonial loyalties and clan obligations might be weighed against one another. While in an ordinary democracy the will of the majority was asserted, in this traditional situation all constituencies were heard and the leader paid heed to all. Yet this did not mean that the two different modes could not be made to cooperate. Notwithstanding the absence of women, the tribal meeting represented a relatively pure dramatization, according to Mandela, of the traditional African ideal of *ubuntu*, or mutual responsibility and community, to which apartheid's exclusions stood in diametrical opposition.

Schooling

In early 1934, when Mandela was 16, his guardian arranged an initiation school for his son Justice, in which he included his ward. Initiation for Xhosa youths at this time meant a retreat into the country with fellow initiates for a three-week period, circumcision, the giving of a new name (for Mandela, Dalibhunga, 'the founder of the ruling body'), the burning of old garments, and the wearing of a whole-body white-clay mask. Mandela's description of this period, which grew in importance to him with time, oscillates between the dreams of a future of wealth and status which the experience sparked, and a nagging sense of inadequacy, of not yet being 'a man' despite being officially nominated as such.

Not long after the initiation, Jongintaba sent Mandela to Clarkebury Boarding Institute, a co-educational Methodist secondary school built on land given to the church by their ancestor, King Ngubengcuka, a century before. As was the case throughout colonial Africa, mission schools like Clarkebury formed one of the primary agents of colonial expansion and socialization, often driven by universalist Christian (sometimes Social Darwinist) ideas concerning the degrees of civilization and possible redemption attainable by different peoples or races. However, there were among them more liberal, independent-minded institutions, including within the Methodist missionary service influential in the Transkei, where emphasis was laid on salvation as being contingent upon dedication and hard work.

At Clarkebury, Mandela soon discovered that any claim he might make to special status as a lesser royal would be given short shrift. Many fellow students, equally well connected, regarded him as a country yokel, barely able to walk about in shoes. Presided over by the severe Reverend Cecil Harris, the school's regime was strict, even militaristic, yet generally fair. Mandela was given a single special privilege as the regent's ward: instead of the usual manual outdoor duties expected of students, he was allowed to tend the Harrises' garden. Here, as well as discovering his lifelong love of raising plants, he opened a unique window onto the private life of a white person, almost immediately after first meeting them: a rare insight for a black South African youth at this time. Relying on his exceptionally retentive memory, Mandela at Clarkebury obtained his 'middle school' diploma or Junior Certificate in two rather than the usual three years.

In 1937 Mandela moved on to Healdtown College, a Methodist senior school, where he matriculated. The school was built close to Fort Beaufort, an important British outpost in the Xhosa wars. To reach it, travelling by car, train, and on foot, Mandela for the first time crossed the great Kei River, a key frontier in those same wars.

The land was laden with reminders, to quote the poet Mqhayi (whom he was soon to meet), of how the 'metal wire' of Europe had strangled and overwhelmed the 'assegai' of African strength and pride.

At Healdtown, youths like Mandela, as well as a proportion of students from neighbouring communities, were trained to become 'black Englishmen' (his own phrase), once again following an austere Victorian regime that inculcated self-restraint and hard work. Their first bell was at 6.00 a.m., and lights out at 9.30 p.m.: their diet comprised bread, maize starch, and water. Yet Mandela took relatively easily to this discipline and found that maintaining it helped him imbibe more effectively what he was taught. In later years he would declare himself always still an Anglophile, a lifelong admirer of English political institutions and manners, though with important (South) African adaptations.

He continued as at Clarkebury to enjoy sports of different kinds, excelling in particular at long-distance running, which afforded him, he said, a stimulating 'discipline and solitariness', to the extent that he continued this sport into his university years. As will be evident from the story so far, the self-mastery that Mandela had acquired in order to deal with his personal losses was strongly underpinned by the strict institutional contexts of his boarding schools. By the time he was ready to become a political leader, the qualities of self-discipline, perseverance, and dedication had come to seem to him not only second nature, but inalienable attributes for anyone in authority.

Intent on 'grooming' Mandela 'for success in the world', Jongintaba in 1939 obtained a scholarship from the Transkei authorities for his ward to continue his studies at the University of Fort Hare, at this time the most prestigious tertiary educational institution for black Africans south of the equator. Although his cousin Justice had until now preceded him up the school ladder, Mandela would from here on outstrip him. He arrived at university wearing a wristwatch and a new three-piece suit with wide lapels, bought for him by his guardian (Figure 2). Although it is now thought that the photograph in which he sports these new clothes was taken at an earlier point, the suit even so represented his simultaneous introduction to the seductions of western dress—presenting himself as a 'black Englishman'—*and* to the most stimulating intellectual environment he had yet encountered.

Fort Hare had opened in 1916 as Native Central College, built on land donated by the Methodist mission of Lovedale. Only two decades on, it had, under the disciplinarian directorship of Dr Alexander Kerr, become a premier training ground for the tiny black South African middle class. Still a Xhosa or, more precisely, an abaThembu at heart, Mandela was now thrust into a vibrant intercultural social network, comprising the representatives of southern Africa's leading black families (the Jabavus and Bokwes), and the gifted sons of less fortunate communities, like Oliver Tambo. Together, they prefigured the black South African elite of the future.

Mandela set out to study towards a combined BA degree in his now-chosen career of native administration, taking such subjects as history, anthropology, and law from some of the leading African scholars of the day, including Professors Z. K. Matthews and D. D. T. Jabavu. He and his cohort were strongly motivated by their sense of bearing special status as an elite who, in the words of Z. K., would achieve success 'through hard work and moderation', as the African American Booker T. Washington had advised. By and large, however, their pride in themselves was not expressed politically. Indeed, their position in many ways depended on their still-uncritical support for the status quo. With the beginning of the Second World War, the students declared themselves 'ardent' Allied supporters, applauding the then prime minister and one-time Boer general, Jan Smuts, the guest speaker at the university's 1940 graduation ceremony, for his efforts in

2. Mandela in his first suit, self-consciously looking away from the camera, readying himself for new educational pastures. In 2005, he observed that he was at the time wearing heavy new boots in which he clunked about like a country yokel.

taking South Africa into the war. By contrast, the ANC was an organization only 'vaguely heard of', seemingly lost in the past, although Z. K., an ANC activist, had protested against the Cape Province's abrogation of the black vote. Despite the fact that Mandela in these years experienced his first openly racial incidents, and befriended people from various backgrounds, both nationalist and moderate, any strongly expressed political associations at this point disconcerted him.

Towards the end of his second year at Fort Hare, a conflict broke out between students and staff on the grounds of the ill-treatment of a canteen worker, exacerbated by an earlier protest over food. This development, which abruptly ended the first phase of Mandela's university career, eventually proved a milestone on the road towards his politicization. The sequence of events in what actually transpired differs between the various biographical accounts. Despite the claims to the contrary in his autobiography, on balance it seems that Mandela was *not* part of the student council that called for an SRC election boycott in response to the incident. Instead, already elected to the council by a small minority, Mandela followed a more solitary road of protest by refusing to take up his position, which prompted Kerr to suspend him. The setback, if anything, steeled his determination, and he returned home to face a furious Jongintaba, who insisted he go back to complete his degree.

A prolonged stand-off between regent and ward was avoided by a second hammer-blow decision probably sparked by the first. Jongintaba, in essence a traditional patriarch, that summer arranged marriages for both Justice and his ward, going so far as to pay *lobola* (bride price) for the two women concerned. In spite of all he knew he owed his guardian, Mandela, together with his cousin, decided that he could not comply with a tradition imposed without consultation. Within only a few days the two young men took steps to escape to the space of black opportunity that was Johannesburg, the burgeoning former mining town, so embarking on the big-city pilgrimage already traced by many of their compatriots, black and white. In the period 1936–46, when the two made their journey, Johannesburg's black population, encouraged by the relaxed influx controls of the war period, had increased by tens of thousands.

Under Jongintaba's suspicious gaze, the two young men organized their escape in secret, selling his oxen to raise money for their rail fare, and blustering their way through pass controls. (Passes were identity-type documents regulating black movement around the country: at this point only black men and not women were required to carry them.) On the final leg of their trip, they were driven in a white contact's car and, that night, were confronted by the revelation of massed electric light that was Johannesburg. Although this seemed like the fulfilment of a long journey, in reality, Mandela wrote, it was 'the very beginning of a much longer and more trying one'. Yet, aside from his sense of indebtedness to his guardian, this step into a new future was one that he felt more than ready to take. Perhaps acting from a feeling of detachment from established loyalties that the early disintegration of his family home had bequeathed, and from his belief in his own capacity to master self and destiny, Mandela appears to have been prepared to sever his lineage obligations virtually overnight. He was keen to step forward as a modern subject, open to the new, independent ways of fashioning an identity that the city offered.

The woman who gave the two young men the paid-for lift from Queenstown to Johannesburg that would change their lives, was one of the first white people, other than teachers and teachers' wives, to whom Mandela had ever talked at any length. In closing this section tracking his transition into young adulthood, it is worth asking how it was that someone like him, growing up in a land striated with white colonization and African destitution, had up till now avoided feelings of racial inferiority and resentment as a black person. After all, both the elegiac voices of leading community elders, and the generalized nationalist histories of his BA studies, had poignantly reminded him of his people's losses, of the pitched 'wars fought...in defence of the fatherland', as he put it in his 1964 Rivonia speech.

A colonial context based on racial oppression generates pathologies in both black consciousness and white, as postcolonial theory describes. This was perhaps nowhere more evident than in South Africa, where a dominant ideology of white supremacy informed all state policy. As W. E. B. Du Bois said of African America in 1903, within a colonial system black people 'always [look] at [themselves] through the eyes of others...measuring [their] soul by the tape of a world that looks on in amused contempt and pity'. For 1950s South African writer Can Themba, also Fort Hare-educated, 'the burden of the whiteman's crime against my personality, negatives all the brilliance of intellect.... The whole bloody ethos still asphyxiates me.' Did Mandela not share such feelings of falling short when measured by the standards of the white world? How did he negotiate the 'system of legally defined and governmentally enforced binary categorisations emphasising, but not limited to, racial oppression', in Sizwe Mpofu-Walsh's definition? In what ways did he avoid the asphyxiating burden of black negation, that 'intense intra-psychic pain'—in the influential formulation of anti-colonial analyst Frantz Fanon—produced when the oppressed internalize the oppressor's perceptions?

The answer to these questions is complicated, but it is probably contained in the fact of Mandela's privileged upbringing in a sheltered rural environment of well-off farmers. His guardian's status more than compensated for his father's loss of prestige, and he grew up expecting to partake in the environment of entitlement and self-possession that surrounded the Thembu aristocracy. In Jongintaba's courtyard, black institutions of authority operated with success despite colonialism, and white institutions existed at a distance for much of the time. As Mandela noted, the regent treated any white traders and government officials who visited 'on equal terms as they did him'.

Until he arrived in Johannesburg, therefore, Mandela, effectively a member of two overlapping elites, Thembu and mission school, would rarely have been the object of derogatory white eyes. At both school and university, his self-perception was buttressed by his membership of different communities of independent black minds. Throughout, within the liberal if hierarchical environments of his Methodist colleges and then of Fort Hare, the students' sense of election was in the main encouraged. In this emerging public sphere, as one commentator noted, they were free to try out a range of different vocabularies of modern progress through which to define themselves, regardless of the colour of their skin. Here, as long as an individual was prepared to work hard, rewards, whether worldly or spiritual, would be theirs. Hence Mandela's often relentless exhortation to his own children to show drive and ambition, and make something of their lives.

Mandela's self-possession was to be tested in the new urban environment of Johannesburg, as when he encountered the segregated tea-tray arrangements at his first law-office workplace. His self-confidence was sufficiently embedded, however, not to be seriously dented. As Gordimer, amongst others, saw, this secure sense of self in all likelihood also explains how it is that he emerged from his years of incarceration without acrimony—this, and the support he enjoyed throughout from a strong network of friends and contacts. Moreover, in Johannesburg, because of the war situation, longer vistas of opportunity were presented to black men than had been the case hitherto.

Big city life

Mandela's first city job was as a mine compound policeman, Justice's as a clerk—positions they secured using their Thembu contacts. The same network entrapped them, however, when an infuriated Jongintaba wrote to have them fired. Through a relative with whom he lived for a while, Mandela then obtained an introduction to Xhosa 'home boy' Walter Sisulu (1912–2003), a well-connected real-estate agent working off Commissioner Street in central Johannesburg and already a socialist-leaning ANC member. The meeting with this remarkable man—always confident and capable despite lacking Mandela's social status, proudly African regardless of his mixed-race parentage—fundamentally changed the younger man's life.

Sisulu, for his part, appears to have been struck by something at once reassuring and impressive in Mandela's presence. On the strength of their very brief acquaintance, he set his new friend up as an office worker and prospective articled clerk in the white Jewish legal firm of Witkin, Sidelsky and Eidelman, with Lazar Sidelsky as his 'courtly' mentor. This work, it was hoped, would become Mandela's springboard to returning to university for further legal studies. His education to date, he now felt, was 'hardly…relevant' in a context where his new cohorts, lacking degrees, spoke better English and were more city-wise.

His autobiography does not explicitly address why he decided on the law, apart from the contingency of having met Sisulu. However, the connection between the roles of native administrator, conventionally a rural posting, and that of lawyer, the equivalent city profession, is self-evident. Notwithstanding the law's limited role in guarding civil liberties in South Africa, the courts presented Mandela with a space where, as in Jongintaba's courtyard, people's conflicting interests, exacerbated by their segregated environment, might be deliberated. Like his Indian counterpart Gandhi, Mandela had already at this early stage developed a marked respect for the ideals of justice and arbitration.

Living first in the non-electrified or 'Dark City' of Alexandra, later in the expanding, red-brick township of Orlando, Mandela was thrown into the thick of the black struggle for urban survival and political self-reliance. (The charged atmosphere of these formative city years is detailed in Chapter 5.) With Jongintaba's death, his allowance (which had been restored following a reconciliation) ceased, and this cast the former ward upon the generosity of acquaintances and loans from charitable groups. He walked to save bus-fare money and wore the same suit every day, yet managed to impress his legal firm with his disciplined commitment to his work.

In 1943, the same year that he began regularly to attend ANC meetings along with radical fellow-clerk Gaur Radebe, he enrolled for a part-time LLB degree at the largely white University of the Witwatersrand. He persisted with these studies alongside his clerkship and political work, often under difficult conditions. Fellow students like the activist Ruth First remembered him during this period as reserved, immaculately dressed, and 'very conscious of his blackness' (acutely perhaps for the first time). In 1944 he married the nurse Evelyn Mase, a devout, apolitical woman, mother to four of his children, who for fourteen years provided him with the secure family base from which to organize himself as a radical nationalist. His many rival commitments, however, obstructed concentrated study. In 1949 he failed his final law examination and was forced to complete his legal training through on-the-job professional practice.

Mandela's growth into political awareness was occasioned, he later recognized, not by an 'epiphany' racial incident but rather by the 'thousand indignities' he witnessed every day on Johannesburg's streets. Following the success of the Radebe-led 1943 bus boycott, which demonstrated the power of mass action, he discovered a new 'devotion' to the liberation of his people. Via contacts at work, he met South African Communist Party (SACP) members like Michael Harmel, J. B. Marks, and Moses Kotane, and was introduced to 'illuminating' new modes of social analysis, most particularly, he remembered, dialectical materialist theories of revolutionary change. Harmel is likely to have talked him through the emerging Marxist thesis of internal colonialism, as it was on the basis of communist hospitality to national liberation movements that Mandela later accepted SACP–ANC collaboration. (In brief, the thesis held that the class system in a colonized context like South Africa was underdeveloped, with oppression being at once race- and class-based, which meant that socialists should forge alliances with African nationalists.)

Though a heckler at communist meetings in the 1940s, Mandela at times attended the Communist Party night school in Fox Street and, some years later, in 1950, put himself through a reading programme in the Marxist canon, encouraged by Harmel. Comparatively speaking, however, Sisulu pursued a consistently more radical edge in his thinking, formally joining the reconstituted underground Communist Party in 1953, which Mandela likely did not. As a nationalist suspicious of the 'foreignness' to Africa of communism, for Mandela a place was always to be reserved at the liberation table for the black bourgeoisie. (This was reflected in his political writing, though the paragraphs in question were edited from the 1965 edition of his articles.)

As things turned out, Mandela joined the ANC at a time of reinvigorated ferment in the organization, stirred up to a considerable extent by his new companions Sisulu and Radebe, as well as the brilliant, passionately nationalist Anton Lembede. Founded in 1912 by Pixley ka Seme, Sol Plaatje, and John Dube as a political organization to campaign for native land rights, the ANC had by the late 1930s become a non-confrontational, if not almost dormant, political organization, whose activities, such as they were, focused mainly on petitioning. A new period in its fortunes was inaugurated with the election in 1940 of the energetic Alfred Xuma. He presided over the younger members' successful call at the 1943 annual conference for the formation of a Youth League based on Africanist ideas and non-hierarchical grassroots structures, as well as for a change to the constitution to accord full equality to women members.

The ANC Youth League (ANCYL), one of the most important forces to shape South African politics in the post-war period, was formally launched at the Bantu Men's Social Centre in Eloff Street in early 1944. Tapping the new spirit of nationalism emerging amongst the African masses during the war period, the ANCYL manifesto called for the African to 'determine his future by his own efforts'. On the back of Mandela's concentrated work in helping to set up the League, he was in 1947 elected to the Transvaal provincial ANC executive, and in 1948 became ANCYL secretary with the responsibility of organizing new branches and galvanizing recruitment.

The ANCYL response to the 1948 victory of the Afrikaner National Party on an apartheid ticket to bring racial segregation into law, was to launch in 1949 a 'Programme of Action'. The group aimed to push for mass protests on Gandhian lines, as Mandela explained in the *African Lodestar* magazine. Confronted with the government's repressive new legislation, he was, like his colleagues A. P. Mda, Tambo, and Sisulu, concerned to put the 'machinery' of African liberation in order (the term was Sisulu's). In late 1949, the League succeeded in its plan of gaining control of the ANC executive by ousting the by-now-too-cautious Xuma in favour of the seemingly more malleable Dr James Moroka, and soon thereafter Mandela was co-opted onto the national executive in Xuma's place. In 1950, he was elected ANCYL president to replace Mda, who had been forced to resign due to illness.

Although Mandela continued to disagree with Sisulu until as late as 1950 over his support for communists and Indians, between the May Day protests that year, disrupted by police, and the subsequent 26 June Day of Mourning, organized by a joint nationalist–communist, Indian–African committee, he underwent an important change of heart. His respect for the high level of organization that distinguished these other groups appears to have translated into a more pragmatic approach to forging alliances with them. This was vividly exemplified in the 1952 Defiance Campaign, launched to turn 'non-European unity' into a living force against 'fascism', in Mandela's words. The development, for which he acted as volunteer-in-chief, is fully sketched in Chapter 4 on his political and intellectual influences.

The year 1952 was a key year in Mandela's career. Even though many local ANC branches were noticeably self-motivated in their participation in Defiance, the success of the mass campaign, and the fact that crowds *across* the country marched *non-violently* against apartheid legislation, gave him a prominent public profile, unmatched by others of his generation. The Defiance Campaign proved decisive, too, in shaping the ANC's broad-church politics for the rest of the decade. In his efforts to recruit support, Mandela felt he personally had developed a new confidence as a 'freedom fighter': 'the white man had felt the power of my punches and I could walk upright like a man'.

The ongoing impact of Defiance

From the early 1950s onwards, Mandela's leadership skills, complemented by his formal legal training and gift for forging friendships across various colour bars, were in constant demand. His comrades were aware that Congress needed a rallying leader figure at its head and appear to have collaborated even in these Defiance years in burnishing his charismatic image. He qualified as an attorney in the same year that he became a public political presence, and joined with Fort Hare fellow-graduate Oliver Tambo in August 1952 in establishing South Africa's first black-owned law office, located on Fox Street in downtown Johannesburg. He won attention for his assertive, theatrical performances in court, which turned the busy legal practice into a commercial success.

> You can recognize an authentic inheritor in the one who
> conserves and reproduces, but also in the one who respects the
> logic of the legacy enough to turn it upon occasion against those
> who claim to be its guardians.
>
> Jacques Derrida, from 'The Laws of Reflection: Nelson Mandela, in admiration' (1987)

In any political action, as several contemporaries noted, Mandela
always worked to reconcile his tendency to gravitate to an aloof if
commanding position with his conviction that a leader should be
identified with his people's interests. This duality is epitomized in
his 1950s formulation of the so-called M-plan or Mandela plan—a
network structure of tight-knit cells devised for the ANC in the
event of the organization being banned. Mandela always claimed
credit for inaugurating the plan (and did in fact advocate it
widely): this accorded with his concern to be wholeheartedly
bound up with his Congress. Yet, as biographer Tom Lodge
contends, he appears initially to have acquired the idea from
modes of grassroots organization in the Eastern Cape; in other
words, through cautious, 'regal' observation from the sidelines.
His prison years would reinforce his characteristic distanced
stance, though it was balanced with a steady endorsement of
open, democratic structures of engagement and agreement.
Throughout the Johannesburg period and beyond, strong
horizontal relations with comrades and colleagues calibrated
Mandela's 'vertical' patrician obligations.

The government responded to the threat to state security
represented by the Defiance Campaign with 'drastic' measures:
raids, arrests, and penalties against unconstitutional action. In
July 1952, Mandela was arrested on a charge of violating the
Suppression of Communism Act and, when charged, given a
suspended sentence for his role in the campaign. Not long
thereafter, coinciding with the election of Christian pacifist Chief

Albert Luthuli as ANC president, a banning order confined him to the Johannesburg magisterial district for a six-month period, preventing him from making public speeches and forcing him to give up his important new post as Transvaal ANC president. This represented the beginning of ten years of repeated arrests and bans, interspersed with short 'free' periods dodging the police.

In 1954 Mandela was forced to contest a Transvaal Law Society petition that he be struck from the roll of attorneys on account of his 'law-breaking' activities. His appeal was successful, but from this time onwards his respect for the rule of law would be repeatedly tested by the state's concern to treat him as an 'unconvicted criminal', to quote from his 1962 trial statement. Despite having been banned, he participated in a low-key way in the agitation against the Sophiatown removals in Johannesburg, all the while coming to the grim realization that the peaceful protests would, tragically, not succeed in beating the government; neither now nor on any future occasion. Not long after his first banning order expired, his frustration erupted in an unusually militant speech given in Sophiatown's Freedom Square, in which he conceded, to the crowd's delight, that non-violence could not overturn 'a white minority regime bent on retaining power at any cost'.

In the polarized context of the deepening Cold War, with the government defining all opposition as 'statutory communism' and cementing its policy of full geographic apartheid, the ANC's countervailing response was steadily to widen the basis of the struggle by consolidating the multiracial, intercultural coalition it could potentially represent. In 1955, this widening took the form of a National Convention entrusted with the task of drafting a Freedom Charter, a liberal-humanist *and* socialist constitution that would sketch the shape of a future South Africa and, it was hoped, ditch racialized politics for good. Deploying the same networks and outreach initiatives as had the Defiance Campaign, drafts of the Charter were discussed in ANC, Indian National

Congress, and (white) Congress of Democrats meetings around the country and approved at a vast Congress of the People meeting at Kliptown near Johannesburg on 26/27 June 1955. Mandela, under his second banning order, watched from a distance. He was by now making extensive use of journalism to participate in the public debate about the Charter and, in a June 1956 *Liberation* article, he endorsed its keynotes: the full transfer of power to 'the people', and state nationalization.

In December 1956, the government responded in its harshest way yet to the resistance movement building in the country by arresting key participants in the Defiance Campaign and Congress of the People—156 in total (including Mandela), representing all races (Figure 3). They were charged with high treason. The protracted Treason Trial that followed (first in the Johannesburg Drill Hall, then in the Pretoria Old Synagogue) whittled the original number of accused down to thirty, and crippled Mandela and Tambo's law practice, as well as the livelihoods of many other accused. However, the trial process also turned out to be interpersonally productive: meetings were facilitated between activists from around the country, and different race groups, usually divided into their separate political organizations, discovered a surprising sense of solidarity-in-resistance.

The ANC leaders' involvement in the five-year Treason Trial process, and their neglect of the day-to-day business of political organization, had the result, too, of creating conditions for the formation of a breakaway group of Africanists. Unhappy about the ANC's multiracialism and the perceived communist grip on the leadership, this group formed the Pan-Africanist Congress (PAC) in 1959 on an exclusively black nationalist platform. As such, the PAC had from its inception more in common with nationalist movements in other parts of decolonizing Africa than did the ANC, loyal to the Freedom Charter's principles, as Mandela would discover. Its finger on the populist pulse,

TREASON TRIAL

The ACCUSED

DECEMBER 1956

Nelson Mandela

3. The 1956 Treason Trial: accused, arrested, and charged for their anti-government activism, and acquitted in stages over the following five years. A tall Mandela is prominent in the middle of the third row. Friends Ruth First, Helen Joseph, Z. K. Matthews, and Walter Sisulu are also present. The famous photograph captures the optimistic good humour of the 'trialists', and the multiracial cooperation that consistently underpinned ANC policy. The raised thumb was the ANC sign of defiance.

the PAC in March 1960 triggered the anti-pass protests to which the police responded, as will be seen, with the venomous brutality of the Sharpeville Massacre.

The demands of his political activity produced dramatic developments, too, in Mandela's personal life. His marriage to Evelyn crumbled, ending in divorce in 1958, and he became smitten with the glamorous young Winnie Madikizela, herself from an eminent Transkei (specifically Pondoland) family and probably Johannesburg's first black social worker. She was drawn by his chiefly style, he by her charm, good looks, and the glittering image their relationship projected: together they shared a love of dress and fashion that to Mandela compensated for her political naïveté. His letters to her from prison, drenched with images of tropical dancing, delicate touches, and powerful flavours, confirm the widely held impression of friends that the relationship was, throughout, certainly on his side, fuelled by a strong erotic charge—'electric shocks' in Mandela's phrase. (As late as 1978 he wrote to her from prison: 'The mere sight of you, even the thought of you, kindles a thousand fires in me.') Winnie already expressed the headstrong qualities for which she later became famous, then infamous, although it was clear she was at this point overawed by Mandela, aware that she was marrying a struggle as much as a man. As with Evelyn, Mandela's expectations of marriage to Winnie were patriarchal and conventional, though he did not discourage her desire to become involved in politics, initially in the women's anti-pass campaign. Throughout his life, he would remain drawn to self-directed women with strong personalities like Winnie.

With the turn of the new decade, several African nations won their political independence from the one-time colonial power, Britain. Against this heady background, the PAC and ANC launched separate anti-pass protests, that of the PAC featuring mass arrests at police stations and the ANC's pass burning. On 21 March 1960, in a southern Transvaal town, a crowd of 10,000 surrounded the police station and the panicking police opened fire, killing sixty-nine. The Sharpeville Massacre became a dramatic turning point, leading to the outlawing of the ANC and PAC, the international condemnation of South Africa, and the declaration of a national state of emergency. In Mandela's view, the parallel PAC and ANC protests had sparked an early revolutionary situation, though he also believed that both organizations had seriously underestimated the ferocity of the Afrikaner opposition.

In the midst of this political storm, Tambo left the country in secret to continue the ANC's struggle abroad, from a London office, and Mandela, imprisoned for five months, was called to give evidence at the Treason Trial. In his first major opportunity for public speaking in years he talked about his different ideological allegiances, to African nationalism, Congress multiracialism, and communism. Thereafter, he wound up his legal practice and condensed the mass movement that had been the ANC around its central 'core', as per the M-plan, to ensure survival underground. Still fired by revolutionary optimism, the ANC organized an All-In African Conference for 26 March 1961 in Pietermaritzburg, Natal, to call for a National Convention of all races to plan a new constitution. A mass protest involving strike action and transport boycotts was called for 31 May, when South Africa was due to become a republic.

His most recent banning order having expired, Mandela augmented the hype gathering around his name by appearing at the March conference in a checked three-piece suit, highly polished shoes, and a beard, the last a mark of the radical persona he was cultivating. His speech, which some regarded as lacklustre, yet which was punctuated with cheers from the audience, would be his last-but-one on a public platform for twenty-nine years. It ended with the cry of *Amandla ngawethu!* (Power is ours!), and gave an important fillip to the Mandela personality cult—as did his clandestine meetings with newspaper editors to explain the ANC's vision. Until his arrest in 1962, Mandela, calling himself

David Motsamayi, publicly dubbed the Black Pimpernel, lived in hiding and on the run, moving between safe houses in a series of disguises: nightwatchman, student, agricultural demonstrator, petrol attendant.

In 1961 the Treason Trial finally collapsed with a full acquittal for all. After years of farcical state posturing, and of skilful legal wrangling by the defence (Victor Berrangé, Bram Fischer, and later Sydney Kentridge), the judges had been unable to establish that the ANC had planned to overthrow the state by violence. Mandela almost immediately disappeared underground to help organize mass protests against the new apartheid-based republic. He would discover in this process an even greater aptitude for organization and spokesmanship than he had before demonstrated. As the ANC's entire leadership was banned, the planned 31 May strike was a relative success though a media failure, the government claiming in the press that it had successfully called off the three-day action on the first day. As in 1952 and 1955, Mandela saw that the state was engaged in systematically closing down virtually every available avenue of non-violent activism. May 1961 had drawn a line under further possibilities for peaceful resistance.

Despite the then opposition of Chief Luthuli, winner of the 1961 Nobel Peace Prize, during the second half of that year Mandela worked steadily through the arguments for armed struggle, as Chapter 4 explores. A July meeting with Indian, white communist, and other allies resolved that Umkhonto we Sizwe (MK, 'Spear of the Nation'—the coinage was Mandela's) should be formed as a powerful instrument 'that would take the struggle to the heart of white power'. Though affiliated to the ANC, Umkhonto was to operate as a separate group, to allow the former to continue as a political organization (though suffering the handicap, inevitably, of leadership neglect). MK would be committed to sabotage, but not yet outright terrorism or warfare, to keep the way open for reconciliation at a later date.

There was never any doubt that the forceful, militant Mandela would serve as MK commander-in-chief, responsible for setting up the organization and appointing staff. On 16 December 1961, a public holiday to commemorate the Afrikaners' 1838 defeat of the Zulus, the Spear of the Nation launched its first sabotage campaign with a series of successful bomb explosions at government buildings and electric sub-stations in three major cities. By this stage, the ANC high command, in close collaboration with the already long-term underground SACP, was operating out of a secret headquarters, Liliesleaf Farm, situated in the verdant semi-rural Johannesburg suburb of Rivonia.

On 10 January 1962, Mandela secretly left South Africa in order to attend the Pan-African Freedom Movement for East and Central Africa (PAFMECA) conference in Addis Ababa as the ANC delegate. As well as speaking at the conference—his paper entitled 'A Land Ruled by the Gun'—his main aim was to contact other African nationalist groups and government representatives, and, covertly, seek opportunities for MK cadre training. His six months' journey effectively traced a pan-African map, criss-crossing the continent from east to north, to west, and north and west again. In Tanzania he debated with Julius Nyerere about the indigenous basis of African socialism. In West Africa (other than Senegal), and at the PAFMECA conference, he experienced hostility on account of the ANC's multiracialism, reflected in his expressed view that Arab Africans were Africans too.

Thereafter, he met Algerian Front de Libération Nationale representatives in Morocco, one of whom, Houari Boumedienne, shared with him the insight that armed liberation movements succeed best when they push for the negotiation table (see Figure 9 in Chapter 4). In London he talked to Labour and Liberal MPs and paid his respects to western democracy by visiting Parliament Square (where in 2007 his statue would be erected). In Ethiopia he began a military training programme, which was abruptly curtailed, however, when Sisulu recalled him to South Africa.

Briefly returning to Johannesburg, Mandela set out almost immediately for Durban, to report to Luthuli and dispel rumours that he had turned Africanist in reaction to Africa-wide preconceptions that the ANC was 'communist-dominated'.

Symbol of justice

At least one—probably more—informers were present at the meetings Mandela held in Natal in late July and early August 1962, still wearing his African battle fatigues. The police were in any case tipped off about the date of his return journey to Johannesburg on 5 August 1962. Close to the Midlands town of Howick, they halted his car and he submitted to arrest. He was then held in Johannesburg's Fort Prison, charged with inciting people to a strike and with leaving the country without a valid passport. At the 13 October trial, Mandela conducted his own defence, struck by the iconic possibilities he represented as a lawyer-defendant, a 'symbol of justice in the court of the oppressor'. He opened with an address questioning the legitimacy of a white court to try him. His 7 November plea in mitigation he built into a political testament and the pedestal to his new international reputation, chastising a government that brought the law 'into disrepute' in its treatment of peaceful black protest. He was sentenced to five years' imprisonment, the first seven months of which were spent in Pretoria Central Prison—where he met the PAC leader Robert Sobukwe, equally as influential and masterful a leader as Mandela in this period—and the subsequent six weeks on Robben Island.

Mandela was recalled from Robben Island following the 12 July 1963 surprise police raid on Liliesleaf Farm, where most of the key ANC and MK leaders were arrested and a cache of incriminating documents discovered. Notoriously, these documents included a draft script entitled 'Operation Mayibuye' planning a guerrilla invasion of the country, and Mandela's African diary. The prisoners were charged with sabotage and conspiracy, for which the penalty, as for high treason, was death. The defence team succeeded in overturning the prosecution's initial sloppy indictment, but the freed accused were immediately re-arrested, and the trial proper began on 3 December, with the state presenting a raft of documentary evidence and 173 witnesses, including Bruno Mtolo, an informer from Durban.

The accused and their lawyers (among them Berrangé, Fischer, Joel Joffe, Arthur Chaskalson) were aware that the keystone of their defence would be in the use of the courtroom as a platform for their beliefs. They realized that they would have to admit to the charge of sabotage, but could—truthfully—deny that MK had already embarked on guerrilla war. Instead, they would have to explain their resorting to graduated armed resistance, emphasizing that war had been reserved as a last resort if all else failed. Mandela in particular decided to forfeit the debating forum provided by the witness box, to present directly from the dock a statement of his views concerning militancy and democracy. This both played upon and substantially reinforced the heroic image his time underground had created. Sisulu, for his part, spent five days under cross-examination, resolutely sticking to the line that Operation Mayibuye (or Come Back) had been a proposal only.

I have dedicated myself to this struggle of the African people.

I have fought against White domination, and I have fought against Black domination. I have cherished the ideal of a democratic and free society in which all persons live together in harmony and with equal opportunities. It is an ideal which I hope to live for and to achieve. But, if needs be, it is an ideal for which I am prepared to die.

Nelson Mandela, Conclusion to Rivonia Trial Statement to the Court (1964)

In his modulated statement of 20 April 1964, oscillating between personal history and political vision, Mandela invoked, as in 1962, the influence upon his political beliefs of his African background, in particular of the to-him-egalitarian structures of pre-colonial African society. He drew attention to the government's intransigence: despite peaceful protest, the 'rights of Africans [had become] less instead of becoming greater'. Throughout, he was concerned to underline the ANC's and even MK's distance from the SACP on the grounds of common cause and expediency, though he did not disavow that connections between the groups existed. Socialist redistribution, he said, was recommended to allow 'our people' to 'catch up' with the advanced nations. He declared himself an admirer of the Westminster parliamentary

4. Rivonia Trial, June 1964: facsimile of Mandela's notes towards a final statement, in the event a death sentence was pronounced. The notes read: '1 Statement from the dock 2 I meant everything I said 3 The blood of many patriots in this country has been shed for demanding treatment in conformity with civilised standards 4 That army is [being?] and growing 5 If I must die, let me declare for all to know that I will meet my fate like a man'.

system. He rounded off what remains one of his most powerful speeches with the poised, now-famous statement abjuring racial exclusivity, causing a sigh of acclaim to sweep through the court—and then swiftly to ripple around the world via full-text reports in the international news media (see inset quotation above).

The state's sentence was eventually pronounced on 12 June 1964. To demonstrate the firmness of their beliefs, the accused decided that they would not appeal if a death sentence were passed. Should this be the case, however, Mandela did prepare a few lines of response (Figure 4). Here he planned to reiterate the resolute spirit of his speech from the dock, commemorating the sacrifice of those who demanded their rights, whose forces were growing, and expressing the hope of meeting his death 'like a man'. In the event, the Rivonia sentence was life imprisonment for eight of the nine accused, Judge Quartus de Wet having accepted that Operation Mayibuye had not progressed beyond the planning stage. Late that night, the Rivonia prisoners were taken by air to Robben Island Maximum Security Prison.

Chapter 3
Growth of a national icon: Later years

Nelson Mandela and the other Rivonia prisoners—his friend Sisulu; the young, politically astute Kathrada; Govan Mbeki, the eldest and a Marxist; quiet Raymond Mhlaba; and the two trade unionists, Andrew Mlangeni and Elias Motsoaledi—arrived on Robben Island for their at-that-point-indefinite sojourn on a cold 13 June. The white prisoner Dennis Goldberg continued to be held in Pretoria. Although handcuffed, Mandela alone had not been manacled *en route* and rightly suspected that this (along with later privileges such as the permission to continue his University of London LLB studies) had to do with his Thembu aristocratic connections, reinforced by his new international reputation.

Since Mandela's first visit, Robben Island had been redesigned to accommodate more long-term political prisoners. A strict, racially tagged, warder–prisoner hierarchy existed within which the all-Afrikaans white warders were distinguished by their rural or working-class origins, and poor level of education (certainly *vis-à-vis* the inmates). Mandela's cell in the isolation section, or Section B, was 2.6 by 2.3 metres square and lit day and night with a 40-watt bulb. The thirty Section B prisoners were cut off from newspapers, radio, and all channels to the outside world. They were allowed very few visits and only two letters a year from close relatives, which were usually censored or else held back. At first, any news mainly came through the conduit of new prisoner arrivals: in 1965 these included Laloo Chiba and Mac Maharaj, successors to Mandela in the MK high command.

From the perspective of mainland South Africa, the prisoners had been rendered in every way non-persons, inhabitants of an otherworldly 'arena' (Mandela's image), with their captors being the prisoners' sole audience. The reflective atmosphere, intellectual achievements, and moral symbolism that mark Mandela's prison period are elaborated in Chapter 7. This chapter concentrates on the chronological unfolding of the quarter-century-plus of his incarcerated life, a trajectory leading him through the final decades of apartheid, into the glare of national and international acclaim.

Nelson Mandela.
Crime—sabotage.
Sentence—life plus five years.

The wording of Mandela's prison identity card at the Rivonia Trial (1964)

In the island prison

Soon after the prisoners' arrival on the island, Mandela protested over the racist distinction that Africans, in contrast with Indian and 'Coloured' prisoners, were made to wear khaki shorts, rather than long trousers. For the Johannesburg gentleman such petty discrimination in the matter of clothes was doubly unacceptable, a two-pronged affront to personal dignity. Over the years he would motivate other non-violent protests at the injustices of the prison system: walking slowly in response to the command to move faster; refusing to call any warder *baas* ('master'). He joined with and led the other prisoners—all hyper-politicized men—in observing a largely unspoken but regulated social contract that knit them together as a community. For the one-time firebrand, even his few outbursts of emotion now became calculated, as if choreographed. For example, when in 1970 he complained to the commissioner of prisons about warder assaults, it was on the basis of the coolly presented argument that the prison system should uphold the law and order it claimed to stand for.

From the beginning, his fellow inmates looked to Mandela as a moral authority and model of behaviour: this was the leader who had coped with flair and competence during his time underground. He, together with the three others who had served on the ANC national executive, Sisulu, Mbeki, and Mhlaba, all Xhosa-speaking, formed a prisoner ruling body, the 'High Organ'. There were, however, strong differences and sometimes rifts between them, even when group membership was widened. Splits emerged especially between the more rigorous Marxists like Mbeki, who saw race and class as mutually constitutive, and more inclusive, mass-support African nationalists such as Mandela, who advocated political and economic reform over outright revolution to achieve their primary goal—the end of racial oppression.

Early on, Mandela worked out means of ameliorating the Section B situation from within, and not only through strategically conforming to its (imposed and self-imposed) rules. Noticing from close observation that the warders were not uniformly debased as characters, he perceived that it might be possible to appeal man-to-man to what he saw as their underlying human capacity for change. In his view, the prison system rewarded brutes for their brutish behaviour, whereas a different approach might produce a modified response.

Once study privileges were granted, Mandela elected to learn Afrikaans in order to facilitate this process. Afrikaans was, after all, the language of many black South Africans—as he asserted even at the time of the Soweto protests against the use of Afrikaans in black schools. He suspected that African perceptions of Afrikaners linked to 'English' prejudices dating from the time of the Boer War, and was, by contrast, impressed at Afrikaner claims to belong to Africa. Afrikaners, he perceived, shared with black Africans a history of guerrilla-led resistance against imperial exploitation. He kept in mind examples of dissident Afrikaners, such as his friend the communist lawyer Bram Fischer, and the outspoken writers Breyten Breytenbach and André Brink. As he presciently said in an important 1976 prison essay about unity within the freedom struggle:

> We ought to speak directly to the Afrikaner and fully explain our position. Honest men are to be found on both sides of the colour line and the Afrikaner is no exception...[even if] this country [is] reduced to ashes it will still be necessary for us to sit down together and talk about the problems of reconstruction—the black man and the white, the African and the Afrikaner.

This perception, that dialogue could be forged between the two polarized groups on the basis of shared feelings of nationalist loyalty, and that Afrikaner support was a prerequisite for reconstruction, represents one of the most important intellectual breakthroughs Mandela experienced on Robben Island.

For their part, the warders in time came to see that they were reliant on Mandela's cooperation in order to deal constructively with the political prisoner community. In this simple but powerful perception of mutual, interpersonal understanding, the ground for the 1990s negotiation process was effectively laid down. The young warders' political education by prisoners was, wrote Neville Alexander, one of 'the great human events' on the island. Even the rebellious Soweto generation who arrived from 1977 was eventually inducted into the older men's principle that the authorities should be dealt with in a controlled, rational manner. Negotiation with the enemy, said Sisulu, need not equate to selling out.

From 1965, the prisoners were set to work in the island's white lime quarry. Sunday religious services alone (including with a

Cape Town imam) represented a break from this 'monotonous routine' of 'uncreative work', as Mandela's autobiography describes it. Despite complaints, the severe regimen continued until it reached a crisis point in 1971 under commanding officer Colonel Piet Badenhorst. At the tenth anniversary of the ANC's last political campaign, a number of Section B prisoners (not including Mandela) were terrifyingly assaulted in their cells. Mandela led a delegation to protest to the prison authorities, and thereafter conditions improved incrementally.

Needless to say, there were few 'public' events to mark Mandela's Robben Island years, though in mainland South Africa the 1970s and 1980s brought tumultuous mass protests, savage police and military clampdowns, and, ultimately, dramatic political change. In 1964 there were two visits to the prisoners from journalists. On the second occasion, the famous, and only official, island pictures of Nelson and his fellow inmates were taken, in which he is seen talking to Walter Sisulu and sewing a jersey, rather than breaking stones, his usual activity (Figure 5). In later years there would also be Red Cross visits, drop-ins by British politicians like Denis Healey, and eight visits from the indomitable Progressive Party MP Helen Suzman, in addition to those from government politicians. Each time, Mandela took the opportunity to lodge complaints about the degrading uniform, poor food, and warder assaults, which sometimes obtained results. In 1967 he fought for a second, once-again-successful, time to keep his name on the Transvaal Law Society's roll.

Newspapers and magazines—filched, smuggled, obtained as study materials—represented a crucial lifeline, if one that prisoners could not, until the 1980s, depend upon. There was intermittent, necessarily one-way, contact with the ANC abroad via released prisoners, and occasional exchanges of coded messages, for example with Oliver Tambo. Although Mandela was by now widely regarded as the *de facto* ANC leader, Acting President Tambo was officially confirmed in his role in 1977. Mandela, a party man to the bone, never ceased to support his modest and retiring friend as leader.

5. *Daily Telegraph* photograph of Mandela and Walter Sisulu in Section B, Robben Island, November 1964, one of a rare official series. The photograph communicates the bond of animated mutual exchange and trust that linked the close friends throughout their time in prison, despite the fact that the picture was probably posed.

SACP member Joe Slovo, meanwhile, had been appointed MK commander (the ANC having officially admitted all races at its 1969 Morogoro conference). There were two or three plans to spring Mandela from the island, but these never bore fruit.

The early 1970s saw marked improvements in prison conditions: hot water, permission to play tennis, and relief from quarry work in the form of seaweed collecting along the island's rocky shores. By 1975, Mandela was classed as an 'A' group prisoner, allowing him three letters and two non-contact visits a month. At the time of his 60th birthday in 1978, probably unbeknownst to him, the ANC, alongside the Anti-Apartheid Movement based in London, established the Free Mandela campaign as a central strategic plank upon which to mobilize across a broader political spectrum. This represented a major departure from the tradition of asserting collective leadership only. The 1978 decision sowed the seeds of an extraordinarily successful global campaign promoting and, to some extent, sanitizing the one-time radical's reputation as a redemptive national hero. The world-renowned Mandela symbol remains historically attached to this movement. He himself later tactically manipulated the campaign to the advantage of party and policy, while also rhetorically overriding it, as in his consistent appeal to the collective ('we are happy'). His 70th birthday party in 1988, a rock concert held at Wembley Stadium in London, was broadcast to 200 million viewers worldwide. His 90th birthday tribute concert, in Hyde Park, formed part of the 466/64 (formerly his prisoner number) series to promote awareness of the HIV/AIDS pandemic, with smaller celebrations in cities around the world. It is difficult to imagine the success of Mandela's post-1990 image as the long-suffering saviour of a no longer racially segregated South Africa without the essential undergirding that these mass-media campaigns provided across his decades of political obscurity on Robben Island, and beyond (see Figure 20 in Chapter 8).

My current circumstances give me advantages my compatriots outside jail rarely have. Here the past literally rushes to memory and there is plenty of time for reflection.

One is able to stand back and look at the entire movement from a distance, and the bitter lessons of prison life force one to go all out to win the co-operation of all fellow-prisoners, to learn how to see problems from the point of view of others as well, and to work smoothly with other schools of thought in the movement. Thrown together by the fates we have no choice but to forget our differences in the face of crisis, talk to one another mainly about our background, hopes, and aspirations, our organizations and the kaleidoscope of experiences in the field of struggle.

Nelson Mandela, 'National Liberation' (1976)

The most important prisoner activity of all was study: this constituted the pioneering, grassroots 'University of Robben Island', in Neville Alexander's phrase; in Mandela's, 'a centre of learning'. The self-discipline of study fitted the internal contract of disciplined behaviour and self-governance that the inmates attempted to follow. At first, quarry sessions were used for 'Socratic' question-and-answer discussions: those who already had a tertiary education taught those who were working towards a certificate or degree. Later, teaching was more organized, and included larger group discussion, and, of course, the independent study provided by early evening confinement to cells. Many islanders used the correspondence courses offered by the University of South Africa, the country's main long-distance-learning institution. Smuggled copies of important yet inaccessible books, especially Marxist texts, written out verbatim at night in foolscap notepads, were distributed throughout the prison sections.

By the late 1970s, Mandela's days were filled top-to-bottom with group discussion (prisoner-to-warder, interorganizational, legal-advice sessions), gardening in the prison compound, and wide-ranging reading. He was now addressed using the honorific Madiba, his clan name. During these years he read realist fiction, Tolstoy, Steinbeck, and Gordimer, much political biography, including of Churchill and Kennedy, the Koran in English translation, the historian Eddie Roux, Samir Amin on neo-colonialism, and 19th-century English poetry. His bookshelves featured such titles as *Elements of Price Theory*, Oliver and Fage's *Short History of Africa*, Hal Fisher's *A History of Europe*, and *The New English Bible*. Although he missed the Xhosa poetry that had as a student inspired in him a 'sense of destiny', he worked his way through Afrikaans literature, convinced that this would give further insight into this people's patriotic resilience of spirit. Despite such seemingly liberal reading opportunities, he was between 1977 and 1981 forbidden from studying towards his LLB—a punishment imposed when his secret autobiography was discovered.

Towards the end of apartheid

Two years into Mandela's period of incarceration, the one-time Afrikaner, fascist-sympathizer B. J. Vorster replaced the assassinated Prime Minister H. F. Verwoerd without significant change in apartheid ideology or policy. Hope for the underground opposition came from an external source, the independence in 1974 of the former Portuguese colonies of Angola and Mozambique, a clear sign that the groundswell of the African liberation struggle was at last moving southwards. The Robben Island prisoners rightly adjudged that these frontline states might provide an essential springboard for MK incursions, but did not bargain for the South African government's cynical ability to make deals with its neighbours, most notably with Mozambique in 1984. They also did not fully foresee the extent to which the southern African shift towards independence, with accompanying ideas of black self-awareness, were to inspirit the voteless masses within the country itself.

In contrast with the demoralized post-1964 period, the turn of the 1960s saw the re-emergence of black political organization in the form of the Black Consciousness Movement (BCM) under the charismatic Steve Biko, and the rise of a confident, structured trade union movement in the country's industrialized areas. Inspired by the idea that the black person should speak for himself (the generic pronoun was unquestioned), and not be spoken for, which related to the anti-colonial work of Frantz Fanon and African American movements of self-determination, Biko in 1968 formed the all-black South African Students' Organization, the kernel of BC (Black Consciousness). With strong bases in (then) Natal and the eastern Cape, the BCM was particularly concerned to address the state of political apathy and abjection to which South Africa's black population had been reduced. It used a range of well-tried tactics, not unlike those deployed earlier by the ANC—meetings, rallies, marches, politicized trials, boycotts. Yet its central emphasis on racial exclusivity and self-determination for black Africans departed from and questioned the Congress's multiracial agenda. Depending on the observer's vantage point, this either made the ANC seem out of touch or the BCM appear 'embryonic and clannish', to cite Mandela's critical if defensive assessment in a second 1976 prison essay, 'Whither the Black Consciousness Movement?'

The BCM's significant contribution was to infuse with a sense of self-belief those whose experience under apartheid had left them feeling worthless (a self-belief that Mandela himself had never lost). Defiant black youth faced their oppressors armed only with stones—as on 16 June 1976 and in subsequent weeks when schoolchildren, first in Soweto and then in the Cape, protested at Afrikaans being their compulsory medium of instruction (Figure 6). Once again, as at Sharpeville, the police fired upon the

6. The 1976 Soweto uprising of schoolchildren.

crowds of unarmed marchers. By the end of the year, over 650 had lost their lives, and many more had been wounded. Hundreds left the country to seek guerrilla training abroad.

In spite of—or, indeed, perhaps because of—the fact that the ANC had not anticipated the action, Mandela in 'We Shall Crush Apartheid', a statement smuggled out of Robben Island, was quick to identify with the Soweto students' action. It was a typically shrewd manoeuvre, which counterbalanced the high command's shock at the anarchic militancy of the BCM-inspired protesters who eventually arrived on the island as political prisoners, having been captured as insurgents. Many of them had been tortured before being tried. As reflected in 'Whither the Black Consciousness Movement?', the ANC leaders from then on took determined steps to persuade BCM activists like 'Terror' Lekota of the wisdom of racial openness, and of the pragmatic advantages of joining forces with other oppositional groups, including the SACP.

The entire anti-apartheid community was profoundly shaken by the news in September 1977 of Steve Biko's death in detention, and the banning of eighteen BC individuals and groups. Although the BCM emphasis on racial identity had for a time appeared to its critics to align itself with state forms of segregation, it was now clear that Black Consciousness had been declared as much of a threat to apartheid as either communism or the Freedom Charter. The ANC in exile, under Tambo, shifted its military emphasis from discrete incursions to a people's war based on locally planned operations, though the focus was still on bringing all allies under its 'revolutionary umbrella'. For Mandela, too, violence remained only one tool amongst others for forcing the government to negotiate.

Not long after the hardline P. W. Botha became prime minister in 1978, ANC bombs were successfully exploded at three separate state installations. The government counter-attacked with cross-border strikes into Mozambique and with military involvement against Cuban forces in Angola. A cycle of ever-widening mass protest and state reaction, including two states of emergency, characterized the 1980s. With South Africa happy to use its long-standing anti-communist crusade in the service of defending apartheid (and Mandela still branded an 'arch-Marxist'), the sub-continent was rapidly turning into one of the major endgames of the Cold War.

Cold War divisions were thrust even upon the longest serving prisoners on Robben Island. In 1982, without warning, Mandela, Sisulu, Mhlaba, and Mlangeni were taken to the mainland Cape Town prison of Pollsmoor, an institution for common-law prisoners, splitting them off from prominent Marxists on the island like Mbeki and Kathrada (the latter, however, was to join the group some months later). This was an important development, presaging a government that might have a different view of Mandela's future role than their public intransigence suggested. Conditions in the prisoners' top-floor rooms in Pollsmoor were noticeably more comfortable than they had been before (they had television for the first time), although Mandela missed the island's 'natural splendours' and the lively company of the other inmates. To compensate, he exploited his new freedoms by embarking on a programme of letter-writing, re-awakening dormant chains of contact, and forging links with newspaper contacts and, in particular, the government minister Kobie Coetsee. Further comfort was drawn from beginning a new garden, as will be seen.

In 1983, Botha established a segregated 'tricameral parliament' including Indian and 'Coloured' representatives alongside those who were white, but excluding black representatives, who were believed to enjoy representation in the so-called independent black homelands. In response, the forces of opposition in the country formed a loose coalition of activist groups, the United Democratic Front (UDF). The UDF, though arguably inspired by the activist legacies of the ANC, was, however, like the BCM, independently constituted. Despite detentions and assassinations, the UDF was to prove adaptive and resilient in mounting resistance to the government for several years, until it was banned in February 1988. Its emergence was followed by the formation in 1987 of the well-organized Congress of South African Trade Unions, while church leaders under Archbishop Tutu became ever more passionate in their condemnation of apartheid. In February 1989, at a time of several successful strikes, the Mass Democratic Movement rose hydra-like in the place of the banned UDF.

Faced with this volatile situation, in which resistance was mounting across an ever-broader terrain, including internationally, Mandela chafed against his prison-enforced isolation. He strongly felt he had insights gleaned over the decades that would contribute to finding a solution to the gathering crisis. In January 1985, Tambo called for South Africa to be 'rendered ungovernable', a move that Mandela, Sisulu, and the others supported if with reservations. In the same month Botha offered Mandela his freedom, conditional upon a rejection of violence. (Mandela's state-approved rival, the anti-socialist Zulu nationalist Chief Mangosuthu Buthelezi, was among those who said it would be ill-advised to let him walk free unconditionally.) Mandela wrote a careful response to Botha's offer, which was read out by his daughter Zindzi at a Soweto mass meeting on 10 February 1985. He reiterated his support for the leadership in exile, as if to quash in advance any suggestion that he might act unilaterally, and ended powerfully by announcing that his freedom could not be negotiated separately from that of his people.

Meanwhile, in the townships, violence escalated to street battles, militant funeral marches, rent-boycott protests, and intracommunity 'necklacing' (in which alleged collaborators were garlanded with burning tyres). A dense pall of stirred-up dust and teargas hung semi-permanently over township streets. On 20 July 1985, Botha declared a state of emergency and western banks threatened to stop bankrolling the South African state, which however showed no willingness to make terms. In September, the US agreed to kickstart the process of imposing sanctions on the country.

The negotiating concept

Signs that the government wanted to keep Mandela alive and well emerged around the time of his prostate operation in December 1985, when he was personally visited by the minister of justice, Kobie Coetsee, and allowed to convalesce in a separate cell within Pollsmoor prison. It was at this point that, as on his departure from the Island, a keen awareness of the need to seize the historical initiative came to Mandela. He appears to have seen clearly that if he stepped forward now, he might succeed in authoring a fundamental turn in his country's fortunes. It was a sensitive decision taken at a precarious, knife-edge moment. To act independently was to go against the ANC's tradition of collective leadership, and its current thinking on rolling revolution and a people's war. Not to act meant allowing the country to plunge further into its present 'dark night of oppression', divided into separate camps, with no prospect of military victory on either side. For the first time in his ANC career, Mandela decided to go it alone: as any herd-boy would know, 'there are times when a leader must move out ahead of the flock'. He asked his Pollsmoor colleagues not to protest at the situation of 'divide-and-rule' which now pertained.

His decision at this crucial juncture, to offer himself as sole temporary leader (though he did contact Tambo to seek his approval), would prove incisive not only for the ANC, but also for his own subsequent reputation, up to the present day, something of which he was not unaware. To the 1986 Commonwealth Eminent Persons Group, formed to map a route towards peace through dialogue, he appeared to exude authority. Yet his situation was often precarious, even dangerous. He was staking his good political name on the new initiative, and this involved him in talks intercalating with other talks in distant capitals, of which he did not have a full picture. There would be rumours, seemingly well founded, that he was selling out, colluding with the enemy against his own people. Ultimately, however, his conviction of political necessity, and his faith in his ability to 'master' or author his country's fate, outweighed his and his colleagues' doubts. After years of enforced waiting Mandela let himself emerge as South Africa's future democratic leader, and as one of the pre-eminent players in the history of 20th-century anti-imperialism.

'If this breakfast will kill me then today I am prepared to die'.

James Gregory, quoting Mandela's comment on sitting down to a high-cholesterol breakfast while convalescing, *Goodbye Bafana* (1995)

Punning on his own speech from the dock in 1985, Mandela uses the universal emollient of humour, even with his captors

Although in mid-1986 the Commonwealth Eminent Persons Group initiative was conclusively negated by South Africa's military attacks on frontline states with ANC bases, the group had however planted an important seed with Mandela. He called it the *negotiating concept*, the idea of forcing principle through dialogue; the careful balancing of undertakings and concessions in order to lay a pathway towards a democratic dispensation. Even as the state of emergency in the country was re-imposed, and full-scale civil war seemed imminent, Mandela during an audience with Coetsee asked to see President Botha and Foreign Minister Pik Botha. This was followed by a second visit from Coetsee in 1987, against a background in which ANC leaders abroad, too, were beginning to have contact with Afrikaner businessmen, politicians, and activists.

Pretoria now put together a team of four, including Coetsee and Niël Barnard, head of National Intelligence, to pursue a way forward with Mandela. He for his part continued to uphold three conditions for further negotiation: a refusal to lay down arms until such time as the ANC gained political power; acceptance of the SACP as the ANC's long-standing fellow traveller; and admission of the principle of majority rule. In 1988 Mandela's ill-health, a case of incipient tuberculosis, again added urgency to the still-tentative engagement. At the end of the year, to ensure his continuing involvement, the state's key interlocutor was moved to a warder's house at Victor Verster prison in the Western Cape town Paarl, of which he was permitted sole use.

Mandela saw that the nationalist government was now unreservedly promoting him for a key role in, as he said, the 'debate for a new South Africa'. He was also acutely aware that determination and tactical wariness would continue to serve as his best weapons against, on the one hand, their attempts to isolate him, and, on the other, the ANC's mistrust (especially at the concession of weakness that negotiation implied). Always a public proponent of liberal democracy, he was falling back perforce on a more traditional, patrimonial style of decision-taking that recalled the chiefly deliberations he had observed as a youth. He found himself adept at the skills that the leader-led negotiation process required: the patient restatement of countervailing objectives always informed by a sense of mutual obligation and shared duty (especially to future generations). At heart, the situation involved the dogmatic, formal citation of conflict in order pragmatically to broker peace. Although widespread suspicion remained, Mandela's assured patrician style is generally considered to have calmed nerves on both sides of the apartheid divide.

In January 1989, the 'Old Crocodile' P. W. Botha suffered a stroke, with Tambo succumbing to the same affliction only six months later. Botha was replaced as leader of the National Party by F. W. de Klerk, a cautious leader who held the belief that apartheid might work as a means of granting self-determination to the various 'nations' that constituted South Africa.

Unlike P. W. Botha, however, he was more open to pragmatic deal-making, especially with the end-of-decade collapse of the Soviet bloc, of which he took careful note. The courtesy call between Mandela and a physically and politically weakened Botha finally took place on 4 July 1989 (six weeks before the latter's final resignation), marked by elaborate gestures of respect on both sides. At the time of Botha's death in October 2006, Mandela reiterated his appreciation for his counterpart's politeness and level-dealing, though at the time Botha had turned a deaf ear to Mandela's primary request, for the release of the Rivonia prisoners. In August 1989, the ANC's Harare Declaration laid down as conditions for the suspension of the armed struggle: the freeing of all political prisoners, the removal of troops from the townships, and the organization's own unbanning.

At the end of that year, Mandela embarked on the first of a series of meetings with de Klerk, in which the latter was, like his predecessor, impressed at the older man's style and knowledge of Afrikaner resistance history. The prospect of his release was coming into focus, though the condition for his agreement was the unbanning of the ANC. Even at this stage, however (rightly as it turned out), Mandela expressed concern that the government might be continuing apartheid oppression by other means. This was through a so-called 'Third Force' operating within the homelands, the fomenting of black-on-black violence. Inkatha under Chief Buthelezi was increasingly operating as a paramilitary force, drawing support from within the Pretoria state apparatus. Mandela would always suspect de Klerk of complicity in this activity, whereas de Klerk, equally motivated by a sense of self-importance, grew circumspect about Mandela's volatility in his relations with him.

Birth of an icon

On 2 February 1990, de Klerk made a significant speech in which, it seemed in one fell swoop, he reversed the apartheid policy of the past three decades, and agreed to release the ANC leader-in-the-wings unconditionally. Mandela himself remained calm during this momentous time, concentrating less on the big picture than on the small details of his walk into freedom. He wanted to emerge alongside Winnie and, later on the same day, to give a straightforward ANC policy speech, without rhetorical flourishes.

The following Sunday, a warm 11 February, Mandela walked out of Victor Verster 'hand in hand' with Winnie, as heralded in Hugh Masekela's song, wearing a characteristically sober suit, his fist raised in the classic ANC salute. Millions across the world, inspired by the polarities of the anti-apartheid cause, caught up in the Free Mandela campaign's hype, curious to see the world's longest serving, long-invisible political prisoner, waited in expectation for hours in front of their television sets, to witness the birth of this seasoned yet brand-new resistance hero (Figure 7).

Despite the disappointment many felt at his formulaic Cape Town City Hall speech expressing his determination to progress the fight for freedom on every front, the newly released leader soon glowed in a more reassuring light. In meeting after meeting, whether high-level or low-profile, he refused bitterness, praised the integrity of his opponents, acted in deliberately self-effacing ways, talked about talks, and deferred always to 'the people's' will. The catalyst of the democratic future had been released back into his 'beloved country', as he patriotically called it, and was setting out to render it worthier of loving than before.

The months following Mandela's release in February 1990 were occupied with a demanding schedule of meetings with well-wishers and adoring crowds around the world, from Algeria and the United States, to Zambia and Zimbabwe. For Mandela, however, it was a priority to thank the ANC's many long-standing supporters, including Castro and Libya's Muammar Gaddafi, and

7. *Time* magazine's February 1990 cover to mark the week of Mandela's release. The artist's impression of the long-incarcerated Mandela evokes the degree to which the world's most famous political prisoner was also its most invisible.

solicit their continuing backing for sanctions—until such time as apartheid should be wholly dismantled.

Another priority was to reconnect with ANC comrades in exile, and to attempt, though with a singular lack of success, to dissuade factions in Johannesburg and Kwazulu-Natal, the Inkatha stronghold, from brutally waging war upon one another. A hidden force in the South African security establishment appeared to be siphoning funds and arms to Inkatha to undermine the ANC. Incensed, Mandela considered resuming the armed struggle, suspended in August 1990. It seemed to him sinister that violence tended to erupt in the run-up to negotiations with the government, as if to poison them (as at Sebokeng in March 1990).

In his family life a different kind of internecine war was playing itself out, as Winnie pursued her well-established extravagant lifestyle, and in private pursued a longstanding affair and cold-shouldered her husband. It was clear on both sides that the long years of separation had corroded the marriage, as they had Mandela's relations with his children, who felt he had been a father to the nation at the expense of being a father to them.

Meetings between the ANC and de Klerk's government began in May 1990, dogged with suspicion on both sides. The greatest challenge Mandela faced was not merely to forge unity within his organization. During a time of deep conflict, and from an inherently weak position, his task was to convince his comrades, many more radical than he, to stay the course of transition, however onerous. A particularly difficult discussion concerned state nationalization, which he continued until 1993 officially to support, in the face of an ascendant post-Cold-War neo-liberalism. It was an open question as to whether South Africa, already weakened by the protectionist, command economy of the apartheid years, would be able to balance social justice with wealth creation within this global system. He and his government were in the end to make costly settlements with international capitalist bodies, in particular the International Monetary Fund, in the form of South Africa's Reconstruction and Development Programme, later modified into GEAR (Growth, Employment, and Redistribution).

Meeting hostility at the extra-party prestige he had acquired, Mandela, in pitched arguments within the ANC, had often to stand upon *both* the moral authority he had won across the island years *and* his patrician status. An unfortunate consequence of this dual positioning was that the authority based on experience and his more traditional status tended to become conflated in his colleagues' minds, which exposed him to charges of authoritarian behaviour. He had repeatedly to resort to entreaties of caution: the ANC, he urged, should count not only anti-colonial liberation but also stable postcolonial governance among its successes—negotiations which themselves formed 'a theatre of struggle'. He continued to draw support from the admonishments of Sisulu, the reflectiveness of Tambo (who in late 1990 stood down as ANC president), and Slovo's remarkable talent for diplomacy. Aides frequently expressed frustration that he appeared to fritter away his energy exchanging pleasantries with a vast array of fans. Yet it was clear that he was motivated throughout by a belief in the power and influence of his own principled position. He was convinced that, if he consistently projected an openness to dialogue and a basic human goodwill, others would follow suit.

In September 1991, after revelations concerning the Third Force had significantly undermined de Klerk and Buthelezi's bargaining positions, a national peace accord was struck. In December of that year, the Convention for a Democratic South Africa (CODESA 1) was launched with the objective of working for 'sufficient consensus' for an 'undivided nation'. However, both CODESA 1 and 2 (held in May 1992) were bedevilled by interruptions and stalemates. On the very first day a vicious spat broke out between de Klerk and Mandela, neither of whom yet saw how much they needed one another, and in June 1992 the bloody Boipatong

Massacre, fomented by the security forces, threatened to entirely scupper negotiations. Mandela once again put all of his faculties of brokerage and his 'credentials of sacrifice' into urging his colleagues to balance the advantages of negotiation against the strong push towards militant remobilization. The ANC Secretary-General Cyril Ramaphosa, a pre-eminent broker of the talks, noted his calm 'brutality' and 'nerves of steel', although he was prone to venting his anger in telephonic tirades to de Klerk. De Klerk meanwhile skilfully re-established his legitimacy with white voters by winning a March 1992 referendum backing constitutional change.

In February 1993, nearly nine months on from Boipatong, the negotiating parties announced an in-principle agreement to a Government of National Unity (GNU), to sit for five years, though this was made possible only through the trading of various claims and privileges over majority sizes and power-sharing. Mandela believed that the coalition thus forged would stave off the still-present threat of civil war. Two months later he was again compelled by circumstances to stand forward as the war-torn country's lone beacon of statesman-like steadfastness when the popular Communist Party secretary, Chris Hani, was gunned down by a rightwing assassin. Only two weeks later, Oliver Tambo died after a to-some-extent unsung career keeping the ANC organized during its years in exile.

Mandela used the credit he gained in the aftermath of Hani's death to push for an election date, despite the fact that he and de Klerk continued to be at loggerheads, and Buthelezi looked set on separatism. The Zulu leader finally agreed to participate in the democratic process only days before the 27 April 1994 elections, an even tardier participant than the Afrikaner Conservative Party. Yet, in November 1993, the transition to democracy was made safe with the agreement of an interim constitution (redrawing the provincial map of the country as a concession to federalists like

Buthelezi). As if to seal the process, Mandela and de Klerk were jointly awarded the 1993 Nobel Peace Prize, though they remained mutually abrasive in public, even in Stockholm. While Mandela appeared to resent sharing the prestigious symbolic platform with an Afrikaner counterpart whom he refused to prefer to Botha, de Klerk was not enamoured of a South African liberation from white minority rule.

The run-up to the first, 1994, democratic elections was as bloody, if not more so, as any period in the preceding four years of preparation; yet the election day itself, bathed by a warm autumn sun, was as peaceful as any could have hoped. Long queues of people waited patiently everywhere across the country to vote, most for the first time in their lives, creating a profoundly moving tableau, viewed with consuming interest the world over, and culminating in victory for the ANC. The day represented a miraculous, resoundingly victorious conclusion to a people's long journey, with an outburst of support for democracy, yet a huge amount of moral energy had gone into its making, on both sides of the apartheid divide.

A fleeting moment when history became utterly important, inescapable, and compelling. Nelson Mandela became President, and the word 'freedom' took on an almost childlike meaning, so magical was its effect.

Achmat Dangor, from *Bitter Fruit* (2003)

Mandela's major political-ethical standpoints in the 1990s and subsequently are charted in the later chapters of this book. This chapter closes, first, with a summarizing outline of his long and influential marriage to Winnie Madikizela-Mandela; and then with an overview of his five years as the country's first democratic president, and those years' long aftermath.

Winnie Madikizela-Mandela

Throughout Mandela's years in prison, Winnie Mandela had represented an important source of comfort and hope—'a real brick', said her husband. She managed, despite the censored letters, to keep open a thin but vital line of connection with political developments in the country. Yet her strictly non-contact visits were few and far between, and fraught with anxiety, inflamed by rumours of infidelity that, though not untrue, were stoked by the prison authorities. In the end, this would be the greatest sorrow of prison life for Mandela: the painful distance from his adored wife and children, a distance which produced the mesh of cool control that would eventually enwrap virtually his entire public personality. (In 1968, his mother had died, not long after her first and only island visit. The death in a car crash of his eldest son Thembi had followed in 1969. In both cases, he was not given permission to attend the funerals and had grieved mostly in silence and alone.)

As for Winnie, for the duration of her husband's time in prison she operated under relentless pressure, suffering almost constant police surveillance, harassment, and banishment. She lost her prestigious job as a social worker for the petty reason of having failed to report to the Cape Town police on her first island trip. A different kind of pressure was exerted by the exigencies of the African nationalist struggle. Despite her relative youth and inexperience, she was placed in the position of having, as she said, to 'deputize' for the imprisoned or exiled ANC high command (though her lack of discipline meant that she was never admitted to its inner enclaves as an office holder). It was her spirited articulateness and irrepressible attitude of defiance that helped her to cope. Especially during her years of banishment to the small Free State town of Brandfort (1977–84), and her 491-day detention without trial, she became a key spokesperson for the anti-apartheid cause and an important political player in her own right.

To speak of Winnie Madikizela-Mandela now, with the benefit of hindsight, demands some acknowledgment of her darker side, one that till the 2010s was often purposely overlooked, not least by Mandela himself. For one so self-disciplined, his obsession with Winnie, especially in the 1990s, produced many moral and emotional complications. On Robben Island and subsequently, he persisted in holding her in high regard as a wife and comrade, even though she did not return this respect and affection. As he wrote in 1970, he believed that the cruel treatment she had suffered at the hands of the police considerably outweighed his own treatment of her. This observation, while it cannot be taken as a justification for her behaviour, does however carry explicatory weight.

Comparing her early career as 'mother' of the struggle with later developments, it is evident that aspects of Winnie Mandela's consistently inhumane treatment by the South African police, including lengthy interrogation and shock-separations from her children, exacted serious psychological damage. Her May 1969 to September 1970 detention under the Terrorism Act was particularly difficult, causing Mandela deep anxiety. She always managed to couch her own 'brutalization' (her own word) in a fiercely African nationalist, anti-Boer rhetoric, yet in this choice of word there lay a certain truth. Many of her crueller acts, including her homophobic vendettas against young 'informers', were motivated by a paranoid nationalism. She targeted those—white people and Indians especially, but also Africans—she deemed to have behaved in un-African (including so-called effeminate) ways. Her wilful disregard for boundaries seems only to have worsened in her later years.

In the 1980s and subsequently, Winnie Mandela became implicated in forms of organized violence the illegality of which was at first difficult to establish because of the untrustworthiness of the township police under apartheid. Her 'Football Club' of bodyguards was involved in brutal disturbances, culminating in a complicated assault and murder case involving the child 'Stompie' Seipei. One of the chief instigators turned out to be the club's powerful mentor. As Njabulo Ndebele later wrote, Winnie, drunk on power, damaged by detention and the years of fruitless waiting, acted at this point as if she 'owned' the struggle. When in the early 1990s she had served as an ANC welfare officer, and in 1995–6 as deputy minister of arts, culture, science, and technology, she was on several occasions accused of corruption, for which she consistently refused to acknowledge responsibility. While her trial in early 1991 confirmed her kidnapping conviction in the Football Club incident, the Truth and Reconciliation Commission (TRC) later found that she had also been more of an accessory to the assault and murder than the 1991 judgment had allowed.

Driven by loyalty, his depth of feelings for her, guilt, and a measure of patriarchal responsibility, Mandela stubbornly proclaimed his wife's innocence long after her credibility had been undermined. Yet even he was eventually persuaded to concede that she had done harm to his family's good reputation. In 1992, he grimly announced his separation from Winnie and spoke of feeling extreme isolation. Their divorce was finalized in 1996. She remained active in politics into the 21st century, and militant, Africanist sections within the ANC continued, till her death, to see her as 'Mother of the Nation'.

First democratic president

On 10 May 1994, Mandela was inaugurated as South Africa's first democratic president in Pretoria, with Thabo Mbeki and de Klerk as his deputies. The vast international crowd sang both the Afrikaner national anthem 'Die Stem', and the ANC freedom hymn, 'Nkosi Sikelel' iAfrika', now fused together in a compelling demonstration of the compromise on which the new GNU was based. 'Never, never and never again', Mandela urged in his inaugural speech, in words sometimes cited as the catchphrase for his entire achievement, 'shall it be that this beautiful land will again experience the oppression of one by another... Let freedom reign.' The southernmost reaches of Africa had at last entered the postcolonial age. In lines that the Irish poet Seamus Heaney wrote for his *The Cure at Troy* at the time of hearing of Mandela's release, 'hope' and 'history'—for the moment at least—appeared to rhyme.

A genial, hands-off style of leadership characterized Mandela's five years in office, which began, it is worth remembering, when he was already 76 years old. The GNU settled down to its task of coalition government with a certain amount of relaxed bonhomie. In May 1996, however, de Klerk withdrew his party from the government, believing he had a more powerful role to play in opposition. In the international arena, Mandela offered the insights of proven experience in helping to broker peace in countries like Angola and Burundi, and was instrumental in securing the release to a neutral third country of the alleged Lockerbie bombers. His stated intention was to place human rights at the centre of foreign policy. He was concerned to encourage south–south partnerships and transnational Indian Ocean Rim link-ups, as an expression of which he ensured that South Africa become involved in the Non-Aligned Movement, from which it had previously been excluded. But his moral authority proved useless to resist the tyrannous rule of Nigerian leader General Sani Abacha, who in November 1995 executed the Ogoni writer-agitator Ken Saro-Wiwa, despite international protests. Nigeria demonstrated the grim limits of a human-rights-driven policy.

On the home front, Mandela engaged in vibrant displays of conciliation and bridge-building between communities: wearing captain François Pienaar's No. 6 rugby shirt at the Springboks' 1995 Rugby World Cup victory and taking tea with Betsy Verwoerd, the widow of one of apartheid's architects (see Figure 14 in Chapter 6). In October 1996, South Africa's new constitution, one of the most human-rights-friendly in the world, came before parliament for ratification. Mandela admonished his own party towards greater efficiency, but nonetheless his government struggled to deliver on promises of housing and new jobs in the face of declining business confidence in South Africa and a tough economic climate worldwide. He was rapidly discovering that it would prove as challenging a task to win the peace as it had been to wage the struggle for democracy.

In his personal life, he filled the sociable if lonely days after his presidential inauguration and divorce from Winnie with glitzy meetings with international celebrities from the worlds of show business and pop music. Although these were at a light year's remove from the Pollsmoor cell where he had once meditated on a unified shape of the new South Africa, they nonetheless allowed him to foster, within global dimensions, the networks and connections on which his sense of personal identity and authority thrived. Whitney Houston, Whoopi Goldberg, the Spice Girls, Naomi Campbell, Princess Diana—all were extravagantly flattered by Mandela in media acts that involved much mutual image burnishing, but probably also represented an extension of his delight in performance, something already evident during his early Johannesburg years (Figure 8). Gradually he drew closer to Graça Machel, the widow of independent Mozambique's first leader, Samora Machel, and a freedom fighter in her own right, who supported him both in the dignified management of his personal grief after his divorce, and in the high-profile, often gruelling work of leadership politics.

Mandela's most notable achievement was appropriately in the area of ethical conciliation: the need for the country to face up to the wrongs of the past in order to live in greater harmony in the future. His government presided over the launch in 1996 of the Truth and Reconciliation Commission, under the chairmanship of Archbishop Desmond Tutu. Modelled on Chile's 1990 Comisión, the TRC essentially represented a national talking cure through the medium of Christianized public testimony. Perpetrators of

8. The World's President and the People's Princess: a strikingly everyday moment in 1997 at the door of Mandela's Tuynhuis presidential residence unites two of the late 20th century's most celebrated public figures.

crimes of oppression and torture under apartheid were granted quasi-judicial amnesty in exchange for a full confession provided they could demonstrate their acts had been politically motivated. Victims were encouraged to come forward to indict their torturers and so, it was hoped, obtain moral and psychological release from their experience of violation, though importantly with limited prospects of judicial or monetary reparation.

Throughout, till it published its findings in 1998, the TRC remained controversial, with the ANC eventually attempting, against Mandela's advice, to block the five-volume final report, which detailed abuses of power committed in its own training camps. Perhaps the most important outcome of the Commission's work was to have staged what proved to be a human drama of revelations, offering a historic moment of recognition of the suffering of the many ordinary victims of apartheid. Although its critics were shocked at the impunity it granted to perpetrators, it provided, through its extensive media coverage, a cathartic process for them to face up to the ills of the past. Ultimately, however, of the more than 7,000 applications for amnesty it received, only 1,146 were granted.

In 1997, after a rip-roaring speech criticizing the ANC for complacency and careerism, Mandela stepped down as its president. At the June 1999 general election that returned the party to power, he formally handed over to Thabo Mbeki, as he had long promised. His time in government had not delivered as much as it had set out to do, due largely to South Africa's attempts to follow the privatizing, neo-liberal trends of the global market and turn away from the socialist principles of the 1955 Freedom Charter. However, reforms in respect of township electrification, universal education, and health care were in train. In cities like Johannesburg, black entrepreneurial empowerment was unstoppable; as, too, was a massive crime wave, unhindered by a corrupt, underpaid police force.

Despite near-universal adulation, Mandela had been determined not to remain in office and become that dreaded cliché, the African president-for-life. He now took keen interest in building himself a new house in his childhood village, Qunu. The house of course had a garden, designed as part of a televised BBC gardening project. On his 80th birthday he married Graça Machel, and together with her invested time and energy in a number of children's charities, most notably his own Children's Fund. The enthusiasm and optimism of children would never fail to chime in with Mandela's commitments to open human interaction and to creating opportunities for national renewal.

In this same spirit, Mandela began in 2001 formally to fight to raise HIV/AIDS awareness. Complicated denials and cover-ups to do with moralistic reticence and legacies of racism had characterized the ANC's handling of the country's pandemic up to this point. Mandela somewhat belatedly, waiting until he retreated from public office, assumed his controversial new role. Yet, once he had identified himself with the Treatment Action Campaign, he worked hard to persuade the AIDS-denying Mbeki government to make anti-retroviral medication available to HIV/AIDS sufferers, one of whom would be his own son, Makgatho, who died in 2005.

In the spirit of historic reconciliation Mandela agreed in 2002 to couple his name to that of the British arch-imperialist yet nation-builder Cecil John Rhodes, to set up the Mandela Rhodes Foundation to foster young academic leadership within South African universities. He remained as aware as ever of the nation's need for unifying symbols. His activities were now streamlined into his charitable legacy organizations, the Nelson Mandela Foundation, the Nelson Mandela Children's Fund, and the Mandela Rhodes Foundation in which he worked constructively with his long-time confidant, the activist-academic Jakes Gerwel. He continued his spirited resistance to the west's high-handed behaviour on the international stage when, in 2003, he criticized the American–British decision to go to war against Iraq. In 2006, Amnesty International, which once had distanced itself from his militancy, awarded him its Ambassador of Conscience award in recognition of his 'fearless championing of freedom and justice around the world', including the rights of HIV/AIDS sufferers.

From 2004 Mandela further 'retired' from retirement, as he put it. His final years were marked by ill-health, associated with ongoing respiratory problems, and frustration with developments in the ANC, as Zuma took over from Mbeki. His wife Graça continued loyally to manage his personal affairs. As his assistant Zelda La Grange observed, he still thrived on people's adulation on occasional trips to public places. The 2010 Football World Cup, held in South Africa, represented a triumph for the country that Mandela had long dreamed of. He appeared briefly at the closing ceremony, having been unable to attend the opening event following a family death. It would be his last formal appearance in public. He died on 6 December 2013, and the queues that gathered at his lying-in-state in Pretoria echoed those of the first democratic elections for which he had worked so hard and given so much.

Chapter 4
Influences and interactions

In any discussion of the historical inspirations that together created the extraordinary figure of Nelson Mandela, he is often placed in a relationship of affiliation with other exemplary 20th-century, anti-colonial, and anti-racism leaders, in particular M. K. Gandhi and Martin Luther King. Then again, just as often Mandela is described as uniquely a product of South Africa's history, shaped by his high-status, rural background, patrician heritage, and long labour against oppression in ways that turned him into a warrior for democracy. In this second interpretation, far from standing on the shoulders of other freedom heroes around the world, Mandela is seen as the primary if not sole author of his story of overcoming.

What meanings made up the millennial Madiba (to cite Xolela Mangcu's 2006 title)? This chapter will consider Mandela's political life as a meeting-point between different cultural and political influences, and traditions of thought and activism—influences that include but exceed patrimonial ideas about obligation derived from his guardian's court, as well as his sense of self-reliance fostered at school and university. It is possible to read his story exclusively under an individualistic heroic heading, as the narrative of an independently constituted identity formed on the road to self-realization through the fight for freedom. Yet such a narrative would miss the degree to which the exemplary heroic life, like other lives, is formed in relation to different contingent histories, as an interface between multiple, at times conflicting, discourses and processes of self-definition. Indeed, in view of the prominently collective, eclectic ideological make-up of the ANC, it is unlikely that a man as identified with his movement as was Mandela, could have sprung into the world as a self-made leader of one exclusive political stripe.

Beginning with the literary and political curriculum to which he would have been exposed as a member of a black elite, the following sections will examine his position in relation to transnational African traditions of political formation *and* his Gandhist inheritance. The chapter will end by considering his growing susceptibility to arguments in favour of active or armed resistance, as eloquently articulated in 1950s Africa by the Martinique-born, Algeria-based, anti-colonialist Frantz Fanon, as well as by revolutionary elements within the SACP.

The black elite's curriculum

Mandela and his generation, including Oliver Tambo and the 1950s *Drum* magazine journalists, were products of a remarkable period of black intellectual flourishing in southern Africa, emerging from the church schools (St Peter's, Adam's College, Lovedale, Healdtown), and after 1916 from the college that became the University of Fort Hare. As Mandela was to say years later, these religious institutions were (until the Bantu Education system closed them down) entirely responsible for the 'education of blacks', encouraging in them ideals of social duty and a fundamentally modern belief in the autonomous self. Evangelical Christian ideas of salvation through good work and renunciation here entered into their 'blood', mingled with the core concepts of a liberal arts education.

Out of the night that covers me,
  Black as the pit from pole to pole,
I thank whatever gods there may be
  For my unconquerable soul.

In the fell clutch of circumstance
  I have not winced nor cried aloud.
Under the bludgeonings of chance
  My head is bloody, but unbowed.

Beyond this place of wrath and tears
  Looms but the Horror of the shade,
And yet the menace of the years
  Finds, and shall find me, unafraid.

It matters not how strait the gate,
  How charged with punishments the scroll,
I am the master of my fate:
  I am the captain of my soul.

W. E. Henley, 'Invictus' (1875)

The influence upon Mandela of his training in literary studies and
the law at Healdtown and Fort Hare, in an environment that was
relatively free of overt racial prejudice, is incalculable. It certainly
reinforced the lessons in moral and communal responsibility
introduced at Jongintaba's court. Modelled on the British public
school, though with an even greater emphasis on character
building through physical rigour, the missionary colleges aimed to
create 'black Englishmen', instilling in their students the so-called
English values of social responsibility and fair play, and the ambition
to promote principled, orderly conduct in public life. The highest
ideals—necessarily English ideals—and the best expression of
character—English character—found their ultimate expression in
Shakespeare. Shakespeare and Tennyson were famously taught by
Fort Hare's principal Dr Alexander Kerr with a vividness that made

their works appear immediate and realistic to his students (for Mandela, especially political plays like *Julius Caesar*).

Above all, their Christian and liberal humanist education fostered in the African elite a vision of a common humanity transcending social barriers, exemplified in the significance they found not only in English literature, but also in heroic stories from the British imperial record, like Wellington or even Churchill. As Mandela's 1990s views on national unity and the possibilities of negotiation suggest, the concept of a shared humanness that overrode historical divisions would return to him with force on Robben Island, sustaining his hope in a future free of racism. This vision was predictably again underpinned by the common cultural text that Shakespeare offered to many of the mission-trained political prisoners, not only Mandela. Using Sonny Venkatrathnam's *Collected Works*, prisoners took pleasure in reading and reciting favourite passages, acknowledging to one another that they found in these plays instances of self-awareness, conflict, and triumph over adversity which moved them and with which they could identify.

However, the stirring expression of the drama of humanity was for the student Mandela importantly not confined to Shakespeare. The young man who in 1938 at Healdtown won the best Xhosa essay prize, always remained attached to the moving cadences and heart-stopping insights into cultural loss and regeneration of the Xhosa oral tradition, most notably the work of the poet Mqhayi, modelled on praise-songs. Here Mandela found confirmation of his still-parochial patriotic feelings for his Xhosa-speaking Thembu homeland—feelings that he was, however, able to accommodate alongside his knowledge of British history and culture, if not always without a struggle.

Around the same time as Mandela arrived at Fort Hare, the leading Zulu writer B. W. Vilakazi in his poem 'Higher Education' memorably spoke of how the 'white man's books' and black praise-songs quarrelled in his mind. It was a quarrel that was resolvable only if Africans were regarded as being as much a part of humanity as whites, a view that Mandela did not hold in doubt, but that apartheid directly refuted. Yet literature, with its insights into the passions and conflicts which move all societies, offered pathways to think through such quarrels. As Mandela found when reading Afrikaans poetry or Nadine Gordimer's *Burger's Daughter* in prison, or when performing Sophocles' plays with fellow inmates, the point where the different literatures came together lay in their insights into human subjectivity. Unlike in law books or historical studies, in novels and drama it was possible to see how the personal self diverged from the politician's agenda.

The canons of Fabian and then Marxist thought that Mandela worked through in Johannesburg in the 1940s did not necessarily undermine the tenets of his college training, though they did slough away his never-robust Christian faith in favour of a more expansive secular universalism. Marx, Engels, Lenin, Mao—all as central to the black elite's extended curriculum as was the liberal humanist's Shakespeare—provided him with an indispensable theory of how revolutionary change might rise from the colonial system's antagonistic contradictions, and about the vanguard role of the national bourgeoisie in such a struggle.

Yet the local Communist Party's belief in the triumph of the human spirit over oppression, its conviction that a people's democracy where 'all persons live together in harmony' was achievable in South Africa, extended and did not negate the values that Mandela learned from Dr Kerr, Victorian poetry, and Shakespeare. As with the influence on him of Gandhi's thought, the diverse social structures and political traditions to which he was exposed created in him not merely a layering of values that might be inflected as the situation demanded. Another effect of this heterogeneity of political formation was that certain priorities and ideals intertwined and were reinforced, most particularly in the vision of a secular, classless, *and* racism-free society that sustained him from the 1940s.

Diasporic affiliation or African patrimony

> [T]he freedom movement in South Africa believes that hard and swift blows should be delivered with the full weight of the masses of the people, who alone furnish us with one absolute guarantee that the freedom flames now burning in the country shall never be extinguished.
>
> Nelson Mandela, from 'A Land Ruled by the Gun' (1962)

Mandela's commitment to extending black self-representation through mass political mobilization, beginning at a time that coincided more or less with the early civil rights movement in the United States, inevitably raises the question of his affiliation to African American and Pan-African traditions of political thought. Is it possible to place Mandela in relation to a network of diasporic African intellectuals preoccupied with ideas of black self-making, of Africans as citizens of the modern world? His Fort Hare mentor Z. K. Matthews, who had studied in the United States, acknowledged a debt to Booker T. Washington's reformist ideas of black self-improvement. And, a more tenuous link, Mandela valued W. E. Henley's 'Invictus' (Latin for undefeated), that was beloved, too, of Marcus Garvey, the Jamaican champion of 'Back to Africa' ideas. Garvey, like Mandela, probably first encountered the 1875 poem in a colonial school-reader and cherished it as a watchword for self-empowerment.

African American thought on racial discrimination strongly influenced the group of educationalists, lawyers, and journalists who in 1912 founded the ANC. Self-made as intellectuals, yet brought up to respect literary and political traditions imported from elsewhere, they found special corroboration and encouragement in African American writing: Booker T.'s belief that education advanced black social progress; W. E. B. Du Bois's speculations on the 20th-century problem of 'the colour line', and the 'double consciousness' imposed by racial prejudice.

Alongside the African Americans and Shakespeare, from the 1920s, South African black intellectuals and professionals also included on their reading lists Pan-African nationalist theories fomenting closer to home, most notably in West Africa. This range of influence is clearly discernible in the speeches of the ANCYL theoretician Anton Lembede who, decades before Biko, invoked an organic, continental black identity, and urged Africans to develop self-reliance by citing Garvey, Du Bois, and Xhosa heroes of the past, as well as Shakespeare. The cosmopolitan world of Sophiatown that regarded all-Africa as the audience for its music and journalism, undoubtedly bore the mark of these influences, of English literature, American jazz, and ideas of pan-African unity (Figure 9).

9. Morocco 1962: Mandela in a meeting with the Algerian Front de Libération Nationale, extending his pan-African connections.

Yet, though Mandela familiarized himself with the writing on liberation of nationalist leaders like Kwame Nkrumah of the Gold Coast (later Ghana), and the widely influential Pan-Africanist George Padmore, he, unlike some of his political friends and forebears, does not fit into the transnational African lineage in obvious ways. He remained till relatively late a Thembu patriot as well as an African nationalist with a specifically South African focus. His 1962 and 1964 court speeches make clear that he saw himself as indebted first and foremost to indigenous, not imported, traditions of resistance struggle, even where African models were being transmitted back to Africa via the diaspora. He spoke of the 'wars fought by our ancestors in defence of the fatherland' as inspiring him with the hope 'to serve my people and make my own humble contribution to their freedom struggle'.

Such exclusive loyalties were shaped in part by the special restrictions of internal colonialism under which a rurally educated, black nationalist like Mandela operated, which meant his access to the major channels of pan-Africanist thinking was not always direct, certainly not in the 1940s. So it was the urbanite Sisulu rather than Mandela who made a point in this early period of following wider African nationalist developments in the papers (and who first read up on India's long freedom struggle). This relative distance from a specifically Pan-nationalist affiliation helps explain how, unlike other early Africanists in the ANC, Mandela became increasingly more, rather than less, open to a heterogeneous array of political influences, in addition to nationalism: to socialist and communist thought, and to theories of resistance drawn from India.

For Mandela, one of the drawbacks of later Black Consciousness thinking was how closely it was influenced by African American and European existential ideas of black self-determination when there were heroes of resistance to admire closer to home: the Khoi-khoi leader Willem Uithaalder, Makhanda (an early inmate of Robben Island), Moshoeshoe, Cetshwayo. The clenched fist salute, too, he was anxious to point out, far from first being raised as a Black Power sign, was used by the ANC in 1960. (Relatedly, his interest in the Afrikaans language lay in its indigeneity; it was a language that had grown on South African soil, with black roots.) On his 1990 triumphal tour of America, Mandela marked his distance even from Martin Luther King's ideal of non-violence as having been untenable for South Africa in the 1960s. However, he was always ready to acknowledge his debts to that other champion of anti-colonial non-violence, Gandhi, from whose political strategies King in the 1950s, too, borrowed. King's struggle in this respect ran in parallel with Mandela's. In his 1976 BCM essay, Mandela praises Gandhi's 'quest for unity' as one emulated by the ANC, and in his biography he describes the prison hunger-strike as a tactic adapted from Gandhi.

Social cooperation, consensual government, community unity, cultural dignity—Mandela's core values as a nationalist, he repeatedly claimed, were embedded in local and regional African traditions and practices, and enshrined in the oral tradition. Indeed, his very assertion of the importance of the indigenous and local is itself nationalist, as well as being modern and synthetic. The value of the local and patrimonial only fully emerges to one separated from their customary background whether by an individualist western education or by an alienated urban life. This recognition does not, however, take away from the consistency with which Mandela always upheld in particular the traditional ideal—also the reinvented tradition—of *ubuntu*, of, that is, mutual responsibility and human fellowship.

Warriors for freedom: Gandhi, Nehru, Mandela

> Passive resistance is a method of securing rights by personal suffering; it is the reverse of resistance by arms. When I refuse to do a thing that is repugnant to my conscience, I use soul-force [*satyagraha*]. For instance, the government of the day has passed a law which is applicable to me. I do not like it. If, by using violence, I force the government to repeal the law, I am employing what may be termed body-force. If I do not obey the law, and accept the penalty for its breach, I use soul-force. It involves sacrifice of self.
>
> M. K. Gandhi, from 'Passive Resistance', *Hind Swaraj* (1910)

Till recently, histories of 20th-century freedom struggles have frequently paired the names of Gandhi and Mandela, as representing two sides of the same anti-colonial, nationalist coin. Both leaders, in the standard interpretation, achieved independence for their countries through largely non-violent means, though Gandhi's commitment to passive resistance is recognized to have been uncompromising in a way that Mandela could not—and did not seek to—match. Moreover, reinforcing this link, Mandela is perceived not only to have shared in Gandhi's vision of a common humanity transcending racial, cultural, and other differences, but to have derived strategies of non-constitutional protest directly from the Indian leader's legacy, originally forged on South African soil. In words of homage dedicated to Mandela after his retirement, whether by political opponents like businessman Tony Leon or supporters like Gordimer, the comparison with Gandhi, and the references to a shared secular saintliness, were often almost formulaic. It was in recognition of this debt that Mandela in 2000 was co-awarded India's Gandhi Peace Prize.

The fellow feeling that flows from Mandela towards his anti-colonial counterpart M. K. Gandhi is undeniable, though hindsight might over-accentuate its extent. As far back as the early 1950s, in the vibrant world of cosmopolitan Sophiatown, Mandela was noted as not only a stylish dresser but also an 'adherent' of Mahatma Gandhi's philosophy of non-violence. Like Gandhi, Mandela from the beginning of his career as a politicized lawyer stood for, and stood up for, human dignity, thereby exposing the hypocrisy of his apartheid-supporting opponents. Like Gandhi, too, Mandela deployed non-violent strategies in order to achieve his political aims, though Gandhi did so more persistently, under less repressive duress. Mandela had a portrait of Gandhi hanging alongside pictures of the Allied leaders Stalin, Roosevelt, and Churchill, and of the storming of the Winter Palace, in his first Orlando home. From 1964 he emphasized that a Gandhist philosophy of toleration had shaped the ANC's liberationist 'school of thought'. A historical parallel undergirds the link between them: both spent periods of imprisonment in Johannesburg's infamous Fort prison (now the site of the Constitutional Court): Gandhi in 1908 when campaigning for Indian rights; Mandela in 1956 and 1962.

However, looked at more closely, the apparent similarity between the two leaders, though it rests on a commitment to non-constitutional action in the name of a higher justice, is complicated by a number of factors (to say nothing of 2010s feminist challenges to Gandhi's reputation). Not least among these factors is, first, that Gandhi (1869–1948) is chronologically and in terms of influence Mandela's political precursor. Second, Mandela is only one among Gandhi's African heirs, and a belated one at that. Kenneth Kaunda and Kwame Nkrumah, too, invoked his passive resistance legacy. Third, and most important, Mandela's relationship of influence with Gandhi from the start entailed a situation of difficult affiliation rather than direct tribute. To Mandela, the relationship was always complicated by the conflicting claims of first Africanist and then socialist

allegiance, and finally by the commitment to 'armed propaganda':
'there came a point in our struggle when the [oppressor's] brute
force... could no longer be countered through passive resistance
alone'. Therefore, when post-1990 Mandela commented in a
comparative way on Gandhi's importance and referred to the
'sacred' qualities of this freedom warrior, he also described him as
a citizen of *both* South Africa *and* India, hence as claiming a
different, dual set of cultural and nationalist ties. For Mandela,
too, in contrast to Gandhi, self-actualization was to be achieved
within the ambit of the heterosexual family unit, whereas, for the
Indian leader, *satyagraha* involved extreme self-restraint and the
decentring of conventional gender relations.

If anything, there are in terms of character and approach stronger
links of affiliation between Mandela and Jawaharlal Nehru,
India's first prime minister, a Gandhi follower, and a partial
contemporary, as a reading of the latter's *The Discovery of India*
(1946) and, especially, his 1936 *Autobiography* alongside
Mandela's life-writing confirms. When in search of inspirational
histories of liberation struggle in the 1940s, Mandela turned to
Nehru as well as to Gandhi, finding in the former a political
pragmatism and strong personal discipline that corresponded
with Mandela's own, as well as a congenial emotive connection to
his nation, India. By 1947, the year of Indian independence, Nehru
had become for Mandela an epitome of the inspirational leader.

The younger Mandela shared with Nehru, too, an admiration
for the rationality of socialism, and state modernization, and
he may also have identified with Nehru's conviction of his
messianic purpose as leader—as expressed in the latter's
autobiography—accompanied by a strong sense of personal
isolation, 'an exile's feeling'. Moreover, Nehru's acceptance of the
principle of justified retaliation, and the frustration he felt
about Gandhi's determined pacifism, resonated with Mandela's
always-tactical, qualified adoption of a passive resistance stance.
On Robben Island, he kept Nehru's—as well as Gandhi's—prison

memoirs in mind as examples of how to maintain mental resilience through the discipline of reading and writing. He was no doubt self-consciously building on these points of commonality when he borrowed from Nehru's prose in his own early speeches and articles. From the epilogues of Nehru's *Discovery* and *Autobiography*, and his collection of essays, *The Unity of India* (1942), Mandela derived some of the governing phrases and images of his career: *No Easy Walk to Freedom, The Struggle Is My Life*.

Yet Mandela's affiliation to Nehru is as complicated by his Africanist loyalties as is his tie to Gandhi, definitely so at the time of his initial influence, but also thereafter. The divergences between the Indian leaders and Mandela go deeper than differences in historical context and national temperament alone might suggest. Even those who claim a continuous line of inheritance from Gandhi to Mandela concede that during his early period of ANCYL activism, Mandela's nationalism took exclusive, Africanist forms. It was noticeable that, within the ANCYL, Mandela always lagged behind his colleague Sisulu in forging common cause with the South African Indian Congress (SAIC), and local Indian leaders like Yusuf Dadoo. For Mandela, the ANC alone was the embodiment of the African will against oppression. Until the late 1940s, he was openly suspicious of collaborating with both 'Indians' and whites, on the grounds that their representatives' expertise gave them an advantage over African leaders 'out of all proportion to their numbers'. It was a class- as well as race-based point. Although the ANC had always taken the line that opposition to white racialism must entail a refusal to assert black racialism, Mandela sought to promote more marginalized black African political claims first and foremost. In his view, too, many South African Indians had found in communism a viable anti-colonial political critique, whereas he as a fervent nationalist was not convinced to the same extent by communism. As late as 1950, he and other African nationalists were involved in breaking up meetings of ANC and SAIC communists—'tearing up posters and capturing the microphone'—on the grounds that communism was un-African. African workers, they felt, were oppressed on the grounds of race, not class.

To understand properly the comparative axis that putatively connects the two leaders, Mandela and Gandhi, it is important to ask what it was, in the space of a few years, that changed Mandela's way of thinking. How was it that he became a proponent, if for a limited period, of Gandhist passive resistance? Here a recognition of the wider political landscape is key. In a context of growing international support for colonial self-determination and of the fight against Nazism, Gandhi's Congress movement was widely perceived as having brought the British Empire to its knees through non-violence. In a 1949 pamphlet, Kwame Nkrumah defined what he called Positive Action, directed at self-government, as 'the adoption of all legitimate and constitutional means...[to] attack the forces of imperialism...as used by Gandhi in India'. Guided by Nkrumah and the Caribbean activist George Padmore, and recognizing the challenges posed by militant resistance, African leaders at the 1945 Fifth Pan-African Congress, held in Manchester, *all* expressed a strong adherence to Gandhist non-violence.

In the relatively closed South African context, another crucial fact underpinning Mandela's change of heart was that the ANC had, almost from its inception, experienced forms of interaction with Gandhist policies, a cooperation explained by Ghandi having worked in South Africa as a lawyer-activist for nearly twenty-one years, in 1893–1914. In Mandela's retrospective words, 'The Indian struggle, in a sense, is rooted in the African'—and this despite the discomfort expressed by Gandhi and his followers at being classed with 'Natives' while in prison. As *Hind Swaraj* (1910) and *Satyagraha in South Africa* (1928) clarify, Gandhi developed in the country his doctrine of passive resistance to imperial oppression, based on a thoroughgoing spiritual critique of western civilization: its materialist ideologies of progress, its 'predominance of might over right'. Practically, Gandhi, first in Natal and later in the Transvaal (the provinces where indentured labourers had been concentrated), organized Indians to protest against restrictions on their rights to land, business practice, and citizenship through symbolic acts of refusal (certificate burning, marches), along with morally committed law-breaking. *Satyagraha*, or 'soul-force', the non-violent resistance to injustice, as Mandela observed in 2000, meant that Gandhi's was a 'complete' critique not only of colonial relations of power, but also of the industrial capital that fuelled colonialism, its structures of economic exploitation, its ethic of self-interest.

As the journalism of its founders demonstrates, the ANC had always been keenly aware of the influential, non-violent operations of its Indian nationalist counterparts. It is interesting, however, that a Gandhist mode within ANC activism was most strongly expressed in its Women's League activities: in their reliance on petitions, marches, chanting, public derision, and mass silences; that is, on symbolic action, culminating in their 1956 March on Pretoria. In the 1950s, Mandela's engagement with passive resistance strategies was consistently reinforced and amplified by ANC Women's League and Federation of South African Women protests. As early as 1913, African women in the Orange Free State had, apparently spontaneously, expressed their rejection of the extension of pass laws to women by dumping pass books at police stations and giving themselves up for arrest.

For any Mandela–Gandhi comparison, this situation of parallel activism involving Africans and Indians is of central importance. In the mid-1940s, as Mandela, Sisulu, and others were developing Congress into a broad-based national liberation movement, the Indian Congresses in Natal and the Transvaal, too, were powerfully organizing against repressive laws applied to Indians. Two of Mandela's fellow law students, Ismail Meer and J. N. Singh, spearheaded the 1946 passive resistance campaign against Smuts's 'ghetto laws' restricting Indians to particular urban areas, so re-awakening Gandhist strategies from earlier in the century. Mandela, who sometimes stayed at Kathrada's inner-city lodgings, Kholvad house, participated there in lively discussions with a variety of campaigners, Gandhists as well as radical Christians and communists. Yet, concerned as he was for African freedom, he at this point (unlike Sisulu) *still* took a strictly observer role *vis-à-vis* the Indians' politics. To him, until *satyagraha* could be projected onto a multiracial platform, it remained identified as a means of agitation for an ethnic minority alone.

What changed, in a nutshell, was the 1948 victory of the Afrikaner National Party, with its explicit policy of codifying white domination and racial segregation as law. Now a proportional relationship developed in the country between the expression of non-white protest and the level of white repression. As resistance grew in intensity, so did the state's expression of its 'formidable apparatus of force and coercion', in Mandela's words. Indian and African leaders, including Sisulu, had in 1949 been forced to stand together to express communal grief following riots in Durban in which Africans turned on Indians, perceiving them, within the punishing hierarchy of apartheid, to be their exploiters. Mandela held himself apart from this joint action, yet the broad front then demonstrated had the same effect on him as his new collaboration with outlawed SACP members, dramatizing that there was benefit to be gained from expressing solidarity in practice. The unforgiving mobilization of the apartheid laws had forced opponents of the regime into recognizing the strengths that lay in mutual cooperation (Figure 10).

In 1949, the ANCYL launched a Programme of Action that involved the deployment of unmistakably Gandhist 'weapons'—boycott, civil disobedience, peaceful marches, non-cooperation (strategies Gandhi had himself cooperatively 'borrowed' from Irish nationalists and British suffragettes). These weapons, it was believed, would not immediately become the targets of violent

10. Kapitan's restaurant, Kort Street, downtown Johannesburg, 2006. A symbol of his growing cross-cultural affinities, Kapitan's was one of Mandela's favourite 1950s lunchtime eateries, where he especially enjoyed the prawn curry. Kapitan's is one of the few fixtures of the young Mandela's urban life that remained open for business into the 21st century.

state repression as would more conventional methods, yet could not be ignored in the way that ANC petitioning had been dismissed in the past. In 1950, the ANC directly cooperated with the SAIC and SACP in organizing a May Day strike (which Mandela did not back), and then a National Day of Protest against the Suppression of Communism Act (which he did). Always concerned that the ANC spearhead any initiative, the June Day of Protest was the first occasion on which Mandela worked alongside Indian comrades and future friends like Ahmed Kathrada, thereby laying the ground for a new coalition politics. He perceived that the 'Gandhian model' did not necessarily demand a full moral commitment but was, for an unarmed people, principally a tactic 'to be used as the situation demanded', most dynamically so in mid-1952.

The massively successful, four-month ANC–SAIC Defiance Campaign was first formally motivated by Sisulu at the thirty-fifth annual ANC conference in December 1951, where M. K. Gandhi's son Manilal was present, in order 'to force the government to repeal six unjust laws'. Symbolically timed to coincide with the tercentennial celebrations of white settlement, the first protest procession marched on 26 June 1952, led by veteran Gandhist Nana Sita, its objective peacefully to violate the state's area restrictions and petty apartheid laws. Protesters walked, singing, into racially segregated residential areas without the requisite permits, and so into gaol. In *Drum*'s description: 'Everywhere they marched quietly and did what they were told by the police, singing hymns with their thumbs up. They always informed the police beforehand to make sure they would be arrested.'

As the Campaign's national volunteer-in-chief, Mandela, with Maulvi Cachalia as his deputy, travelled the country, mainly on trains, recruiting both new and more established constituencies of supporters. For the first time he learned about his own capacity for mass outreach, for persuading protesters to remain consistent in their non-violence (which was fundamental to the

Campaign's success). He came to realize, as had Gandhi on his many railway journeys across India, that the reach of inspirational leadership can be measured through the number and power of the symbolic goals it sets.

The collaborative Defiance Campaign remains a major success in the ANC's historical annals. Over 8,500 defiers of all races came forward, leading to a total of 2,354 arrests. Congress was turned into a mass movement based in passive resistance with a burgeoning membership. Cross-nationalist and intermovement cooperation, and the symbolic eloquence of non-violent protest— singing, marching, dancing—was never more persuasively demonstrated in South Africa than at this point. The mass mobilization had allowed the ANC to maintain a moral advantage, yet it also instilled in its members a sense of agency and comradeship. As for Mandela, due to a series of banning orders in the decade that followed, he was never again, until his release from prison forty years later, so publicly associated with a particular activist line. An important indication of how central the advocacy of peaceful protest became to ANC politics and rhetoric is that in 1969, long after Sharpeville, the ANC journal *Sechaba* felt obliged to cite an obscure 1938 Declaration on the defence of rights by Gandhi to justify the turn to armed struggle. 'Violence', he had there noted, was preferable to 'the emasculation of a whole race'.

The narrative of political influence connecting Mandela to Gandhi can be concentrated down to the following areas of borrowing and linked activity. First, as regards their role and style as leaders, both Gandhi and Mandela, though at different historical moments, powerfully channelled in their respective countries the great wave of anti-imperial activity that from the First World War had begun to change the geopolitical map. They did so, first and foremost, by working to create *popular mass movements* in which they eclectically deployed, at one and the same time, not only the peaceable aspects of indigenous cultures (weaving, tactics of communal discussion), but also, equally, modern media technologies and the power of the image. Both were shrewd exploiters of their own myth, to the extent that even the inner, private spaces of their lives were turned outwards to the public in service of the myth. Like Gandhi, Mandela delighted in using the language of dress (less so the language of the body) to symbolize his politics, as will be seen. In this, however, it was not so much that he learned from Gandhi *per se*, as that he developed, through his prison years, his youthful delight in sartorial display into an almost intuitive, postmodern-seeming sensitivity to the media image. Fatima Meer once flippantly commented: 'Gandhi took off his clothes. Nelson *loves* his clothes.'

Then, though both Gandhi and Mandela worked *against* the Victorian (and then Edwardian) empire and its aftermath, both men, too, were in certain ways its products. They were schooled as *black Englishmen* within empire's educational institutions and trained as lawyers within its legal systems. In consequence, both were shaped by the complicated conjunctions of social pathways and political pilgrimages that empire generated, and felt the impact of, as Edward Said writes, the dynamic cultural activity such conjunctions unleashed. Despite Gandhi's outright rejection of modern civilization, he shared with Mandela a respect for British traditions of justice and democracy, and an appreciation of aspects of European culture, especially of the great books of the liberal west. Gandhi emotively cited Tennyson to persuade the British to Quit India; Mandela recited Henley by way of self-motivation in prison. Both espoused the quintessentially Victorian virtues of self-help and self-reliance.

Furthermore, as part of their *humanizing vision*, both had the ability (Mandela the more so after his release) eclectically to synthesize counter-cultural and counter-hegemonic strategies with dominant concepts and views, as the situation demanded. As an illustration, Gandhi and Mandela, who both found themselves pitted against the forces of Boer nationalism, in 1899–1900 and

1948–90 respectively, discerned in the Boer's determined, often symbolic, resistance to empire important lessons for their own political struggles. From the time that he took up armed resistance, Mandela, for example, would quote as an authority *Commando* (1929), the war memoir of the Boer guerrilla Denys Reitz.

Finally, among the most striking areas of commonality is the willingness in the cases of both Gandhi and Mandela to forge links of solidarity with other nationalist groups, that is, to translate their political relations from a hierarchical onto a lateral or *fraternal axis*. While Gandhi adopted the Irish nationalists' use of boycott, Mandela and Sisulu, borrowing from the SAIC's tactics of non-cooperation, discovered the boost to morale and strategy that emerged from anti-colonialist hand-holding. As Mandela later acknowledged from prison, it was important that exclusive forms of nationalism give way to the recognition of the *brotherhood of nations*. He and his fellow activists were in this respect in the advantageous position of encountering Gandhist activism as an on-site resource, a living, working practice in South Africa. In an instance of perhaps the closest 'cheek-by-jowl' collaboration that anti-colonial history has yet seen, they developed passive resistance in association with activists who themselves had worked with Gandhi, and so moved at once tactically and symbolically against the state's segregationist logic.

The main divergence between Mandela's and Gandhist politics rises, of course, out of their contrasting views on armed struggle. Whereas Gandhi rejected violence out of hand, Mandela grew keenly aware as the 1950s wore on that Gandhist passive resistance had become untenable in an increasingly more authoritarian South Africa. A new ideological and strategic departure was called for, especially after Sharpeville. In so far as an African's life outside the tribal homelands had been rendered unlawful by definition, the recourse to violence increasingly appeared as a legitimate right.

Yet ultimately the link between Gandhi and Mandela lies not so much in the obvious area of passive resistance as in their opportunistic, tactical, and always media-savvy response to circumstance, informed by an eclectic range of political and philosophical influences. Neither was at any point consistent in their responses, unless it was in their emphasis on *self-restraint*, that supremely Victorian quality of self-mastery and operation within the rule of law which they derived from the British colonial education they shared.

The move to armed struggle

> What is the real nature of this violence? We have seen that it is the intuition of the colonized masses that their liberation must, and can only, be achieved by force.
>
> Frantz Fanon, from 'Concerning Violence', *The Wretched of the Earth* (1961)

Nelson Mandela and the ANC made their commitment to armed struggle in the early 1960s because it appeared that other modes of resistance, to which they in principle remained committed, had closed down. Peaceful protest had proved powerless against an authority quick to the trigger and impervious to world opinion. In June 1961, Mandela captured this restriction of resistance options with a traditional proverb: 'the attacks of the wild beast cannot be averted with only bare hands'.

To guide his organization in making its difficult decision, Mandela read widely in the literature on war and revolution available to him, including Mao Tse-tung, Louis Taruc, and Clausewitz. Yet in the various biographical accounts of this time there is one glaring omission from the reading list: the name of the Paris-trained Martiniquan Frantz Fanon, easily the most influential post-1950 theorist of anti-colonial violence, who had already drawn wide attention in Francophone Africa.

To the ANC, the Algerian freedom struggle against the local white settler regime had for some time been perceived to exhibit strong parallels with South Africa's. During his African travels, Mandela came into contact with Front de Libération Nationale officials (Figure 9) who had fought for, and recently won, the independence of Algeria, for whose left wing Fanon had served as spokesperson. At Oujda in Morocco, an Algerian military base close to the border, he heard Ahmed Ben Bella the guerrilla leader, soon to be first president of an independent Algeria, rally his troops and call for the fight against imperialism to be expanded across Africa. In this context, though Mandela never mentions Fanon by name, it is difficult to believe that he did not feel in some capacity the transformative force of Fanon's ideas.

The shift from passive to active resistance in Mandela is often described in terms suggesting a move from a Gandhist position to a greater proximity to Fanon's. The latter's approach to the overthrow of imperial power, based on his time working as a psychiatrist in revolutionary Algeria, was bracingly combative: the colonized, he believed, should resist the colonizer to the death, with violence; their entire sensibility should be focused on this rejection. For Gandhi, by contrast, repelling the colonizer with force was to stoop to their techniques of oppression. These two opposing traditions of resistance theory, respectively advocating non-cooperation and armed overthrow, bifurcate postcolonial thinking to this day. The question here is whether Mandela saw the distinction between the traditions as clear-cut, and, specifically, whether his radicalization was supported by any actual influence from Fanon. Certainly, ten years on from the ANC's move to arms, Steve Biko's BCM, with its outright rejection of white values, demonstrated a clear debt to Fanon's ideas. Inspired by concepts of black pride and resistance to the white gaze, as articulated in *Black Skin, White Masks*, and by his anti-colonial manifesto *The Wretched of the Earth*, Biko galvanized black youth by urging them to set aside negative thoughts, grasp their political identity, and attain their 'envisaged self'.

When, in early 1962, Mandela canvassed prevailing ideas on military resistance across the African continent, he was *already* convinced that the only remaining recourse for South Africa's marginalized majority was violent retaliation. The path towards this decision had been difficult, necessitating delicate negotiations with Gandhist and Christian ANC leaders, but after Sharpeville and the May 1961 suppression of the national strike, Mandela saw no alternative. The ANC's arsenal of non-cooperative responses had been exhausted. Moreover, with the formation of the PAC, it was important to offer leadership to the ANC's more militant groupings, and appeal to their frustrations. As MK's admirably restrained 16 December 1961 manifesto put it: 'The time comes in the life of any nation when there remain only two choices: submit or fight. That time has now come in South Africa.' Non-violent resistance would still be propagated by the ANC, but it would now be complemented with a graduated programme of armed resistance, led by a group separate from, though affiliated to, the parent body. Small cadres of saboteurs would be able to move against the state with greater dexterity than a peacefully marching crowd.

In his first international speech, 'A Land Ruled by the Gun', given at the January 1962 PAFMECA (later OAU) conference in Addis Ababa, Mandela sought to justify the ANC's controversial turn to violence, its 'sharpening' of its 'less effective' political weapons (while reassuring African supporters that civil disobedience would continue). Like Fanon in *his* polemical address in support of anti-colonial resistance given to the 1958 All-Africa People's Conference, Mandela, an admirer of *Julius Caesar*, gave a careful exposition of the stages of increasing violence the African majority had suffered. He suggested, as had Fanon, that the colonial 'atmosphere of violence' was the creation of the colonizer alone, and that in this situation the colonized had no choice but to reject the system absolutely. Any compromise or attempt to come to terms would simply reinforce oppression: 'only violence pays'. Mandela's summary of South Africa's anti-imperialist struggle built gradually towards a short, uncompromising paragraph encapsulating the injunction that 'hard and swift blows' needed *now* to be delivered. Strategically framed as a response to a Mark-Antony-like rhetorical question concerning the role freedom movements should take against the state's 'multiple onslaughts'—'Can anyone, therefore, doubt the role that the freedom movements should play in view of this hideous conspiracy?'—Mandela's charged language was at this point distinctly reminiscent of Fanon's. The latter's 1958 speech, given as a riposte to Kwame Nkrumah's influential advocacy of Positive Action stopping short of violence, had been unequivocal in making its central point: the native's violence was not merely necessary but self-transforming. (The speech, which cited Sharpeville as a reminder of colonialism's murderous excesses, was developed into the chapter 'Concerning Violence' that forms the core of *The Wretched of the Earth*.)

Published in French, a language Mandela could not read, *The Wretched of the Earth* did not appear in English translation till 1965, by which time he was already in prison. Yet, as these parallels suggest, it seems likely that he would on more than one occasion on his African tour, most probably in Addis Ababa as well as Morocco, have been exposed to Fanon's ideas, even if at several removes. He explicitly referred both to the 1958 conference and to Nkrumah's defensive 1960 Positive Action conference in 'A Land Ruled by the Gun'. He would have known about the debates that had taken place at both venues. In this context it seems fitting that MK with Mandela at its head was established in 1961, the year of publication of *The Wretched of the Earth*.

Though Mandela would not cease privately to believe that active resistance had in practice to be calibrated against the passive, at this point in the early 1960s he would have agreed with Fanon, had they met, that colonial brutality had exhausted the options available in non-violence. Sharpeville cropped up in his conference talk, too, as a graphic example of such brutality.

Retaliatory violence had become for Mandela the primary (for Fanon, the only) means of obliterating the Manichean, us v. them politics of the repressive state. The binary choice was to 'submit or fight', yet to submit effectively meant cancelling one's nationalist impulses, which was unthinkable. The alternative was to resort to a self-defining, disciplined counter-violence.

*   *   *

Taking a chronological view of his career across five decades, 1950 to 2000 and his retirement, we see Mandela tracing an ideological parabola away from his early Gandhist phase, towards a support for armed resistance, and then, at the last, turning back to non-violent ideas of political negotiation and compromise. As this suggests, within a postcolonial framework he represents an interesting point of encounter between two, apparently opposed, approaches to resistance: Fanon's advocacy of cathartic violence and Gandhi's promotion of non-cooperation, the weapons of the weak. In so far as he lived through two political lifetimes, the optimistic era of postcolonial independence and the more pessimistic, post-Cold War period of capitulation to global capitalism, Mandela essentially experienced the differential impact of these two approaches at first hand and at times played them off against one another: now speaking of African self-expression by means of the destruction of the colonizer's world; now supporting national self-realization through the embrace and incorporation of that world.

From the perspective of 1961, Mandela's willingness to espouse armed struggle appears, by definition, to represent a clean break away from his mid-career pacifism. Yet there is another way of casting this change of heart. If anything, Mandela's anti-colonial and anti-racist positions across his long career represent sliding points on his ideological scale. To appreciate this fully, it is again worth bearing in mind that active and passive modes of resistance generally work interdependently as strategies and therefore are best assessed comparatively, in relation to one another. As an illustration, Gandhi viewed *satyagraha* as active, far from passive: to him it was performative, energized, relentless; passive only in the sense of not involving arms.

As for Mandela, he and the other more radical ANC members were always intensely pragmatic about the uses of militancy. In many ways they had to be: though opinion differs, MK was rarely an effective guerrilla force. Members were keenly aware, more so than Gandhi perhaps allowed, that non-violence historically operated in dialectical tandem with outbreaks of violence, or what was called armed propaganda: the presentation, at least, of a front of armed resistance. In short, Mandela's move to armed struggle entailed a tacit recognition that non-cooperation could not thrive as a politics without the accompaniment of some form of militancy.

Throughout, there was a determined logic to Mandela's position. In his Treason Trial defence, he made clear that the ANC's defiance campaigns were intended to persuade the government to agree, 'Let's talk'. Thirty years on, he continued to see a firm stance on armed resistance as a means of moving to the negotiation table while, at the same time, his shift towards a dialogic ethic never involved a complete renunciation of political violence. Indeed, it can be argued that a key reason why South Africa did not in the 1980s become the 'bloodbath' that Mandela feared it might was because the ANC was tireless in playing the threat of violence against non-violence in mounting its opposition. Its struggle was 'multi-targeted', as Mandela explained in London as far back as 1962.

Yet to trace Gandhist or Fanonist, African American or Nkrumah-esque influences on Mandela's political philosophy should not imply that his thought was merely belated or repetitive. Influence translated from other cultural and political contexts can often produce creative interaction, rather than what is called a derivative discourse. As in his sartorial displays, or his espousal of

African-style negotiation, there was much in Mandela that appeared to have the mark of something from elsewhere (be it *ahimsa*/non-violence or multiculturalism), but was always suggestively combined with more local practices. What was particularly innovative about his, say, Gandhist or Nehruvian approach, was that he was able to adapt it to suit South African conditions. Moreover, there was much in that which influenced him that he did not find congenial and did not take on board, such as the strong anti-white feeling that characterized 1960s African nationalism, or, as will be seen, Gandhi's feminization of resistance politics.

Chapter 5
Sophiatown sophisticate

In Soweto poet Oswald Mtshali's 'The Detribalised', the fast-living *tsotsi* or gangster, the subject of the poem, who 'hails from Sophiatown | Or Alexandra', is said to 'know' imprisoned Mandela and Sobukwe but to care less. The poem is included in *Halala Madiba* (2006), an anthology of poems generally in praise of Mandela, apart from this one. Yet the apparent incongruity is appropriate. It emphasizes a central though sometimes neglected part of Mandela's socio-political formation, his coming-to-maturity in the exhilarating spaces of South Africa's largest city Johannesburg, lodestar of go-getting Africans: the townships of Alexandra and Orlando where he lived, and Fordsburg and Sophiatown where he socialized.

The culturally mixed environment of 1950s Kofifi or Sophiatown, its 'swarming, cacophonous, strutting' inner-city streets, and the intellectual flowering that took place there, was arguably as important to Mandela's make-up as Gandhi's *satyagraha*, or the militant nationalism of post-war Africa. It was here, in an environment self-consciously modelled on 1920s 'Renaissance' Harlem, where penny-whistle jazz and Africanized movie slang rang out all night long from the *shebeens*, that Mandela was exposed to the social flexibility and creative collisions—the non-hierarchical, discrepant attachments—that marked African

colonial modernity. It was here that he became the master of what
we might now term postmodern display.

City streets

> The undying spirit of the mining town, born of large freedoms and
> given to flamboyant forms of expression.
>
> Herman Charles Bosman, from 'Johannesburg Riots' (1945)

At the cosmopolitan crossing point between trans-Atlantic
influences and liberal mission-school values that was mid-century
black Johannesburg, Mandela acquired the public demeanour—the
eloquence, street savvy, and smart suits—that allowed him, a rural
youth, to remake himself as a gentleman and a citizen. The
cultural vibrancy in particular of Sophiatown communicated itself
through the whole of Johannesburg, including densely packed
Orlando, at the heart of today's Soweto. Here, in crowded streets
of small brick houses, Mandela adopted the 'Edwardian' style for
which in the 1990s he became famous—the pressed clothes,
correct manners, and modulated public speech—and fused these
with the self-control of his school upbringing. In these streets he
developed the vision of positive success—that Africans belonged to
the modern state and the future—that sustained him across his
prison years.

Here, too, he was exposed not only to compelling images of African
American self-assertion from film and jazz, but also to the edgy
defensiveness of African nationalist machismo more generally. The
aristocratic country boy discovered the intoxicating charge of
projecting a modern urban image that was based on professional
shine and outward show yet relatively little wealth. Here, finally, in
the crucible that was freehold Alexandra-Orlando-Sophiatown
before 1950s segregationist laws fully took hold, before apartheid
became shrewd and brutal, the non-combative multiracialism and

interculturalism of the ANC was alchemized. Although this context is relatively neglected in biographies keen to emphasize his patrician background and Methodist upbringing as key factors shaping Mandela's outlook, the 'match' between the cultural vibrancy of urbanizing Africa and the debonair young lawyer tempts further exploration. It is definitely indicative that in the early 1950s Mandela above other prominent Africans became the figure promoted by *Drum* magazine and its white editorship as the embodiment of Congress politics.

Even more than the African residential areas of Alexandra or Orlando, or the Indian-and-Coloured suburb of Fordsburg, the glamorous if seedy Sophiatown of the 1950s, epicentre of urban South Africa, was a uniquely innovative, interactive place, twanging with short-fuse optimism and creative energy, especially in music and journalism. Pastimes of choice were street-side gambling, live jazz, street shoot-outs, ballroom dancing—in which Mandela and many others participated—and, most glamorous and street-wise of all, boxing, his sport of choice (Figure 11). This unifying culture was made possible by Kofifi's 'black spot' status: until the Group Areas Act and the forced removals of the mid-1950s, it was a township where black Africans could, unusually, own property and gain access to a variety of cultural channels, Asian and diasporic African alike. The slums that Alan Paton condemned in his classic *Cry, the Beloved Country* (1949) as a cesspit of prostitution and gang violence, the ruin of the 'true' rural African, were located here, yet what he overlooked about the society was its remarkable openness and resourcefulness. Urban life, as Mandela himself acknowledged, abraded tribal differences.

At Sophiatown parties, white journalists famously mingled with black poets and Indian film critics. On its pavements, philosophers rubbed shoulders with pickpockets and businessmen. In their music, the Jazz Maniacs and the African Ink Spots, and solo artists like Isaac Nkosi and Dolly Rathebe,

11. Mandela engaged in one of his favourite activities, sparring with Jerry Moloi in a photograph taken for *Drum* magazine, though eventually not used. Boxing gave him valuable lessons in the interplay between aggression and defence, which were to stand him in good stead during his time as chief ANC negotiator. The photo was taken not at his Orlando gym, but on the rooftop of the South African Associated Newspapers offices.

paid tribute to African American performers: Count Basie, Duke Ellington, Louis Armstrong. The small black middle class lived cheek-by-jowl not only with factory workers but also a criminal underclass, called the African aristocracy, whose conspicuous consumption represented a bold defiance of township squalor. At this time of pass restrictions, most urban Africans operated, perforce, on the wrong side of the law: denied basic facilities, many believed that achievement was measured in a glitzy look or style. Mandela as a lawyer-in-training, an incarnation of community aspirations, felt the social imperative of wearing elegant three-piece Markhams suits. With his charisma and intense responsiveness to others, he grew keenly aware of the people's hunger for rallying symbols of their leaders.

Almost all reminiscences of the Sophiatown period testify to its cultural syncretism and extraordinary spirit. 'Sophiatown [had] all the exuberant youth of Shakespeare's London', wrote *Drum* editor Anthony Sampson. 'Over our dead bodies' was a slogan of the 1954–5 anti-eviction campaign. The zestful mingling that was Kofifi and its surroundings became fundamental to how Mandela presented himself: that is, to the many-sided political personality this one-time exclusivist nationalist projected, *and* to his knowledge of what *being* a personality involved. In Sophiatown and Fordsburg he gained insight into both cultural mixedness and its performance. He saw how, for the duration of a *shebeen* evening in Back of the Moon or 39 Steps, or at a jazz show by Dollar Brand or Dudu Pukwana at Uncle Joe's café, the divides of apartheid were briefly transcended, their leakiness exploited. Meetings across the colour bar, whether casual or professional, private or political, were buoyed both by the daring they represented and by a heady post-war idealism, a conviction that social harmony was possible, even in South Africa; indeed, that African leaders could remake the colonial state.

The making of a modern man

On arrival in Johannesburg, the youth who had been happy to press his well-dressed guardian's trousers and pleased at his gift of a striped, double-breasted suit, was struck by the glamour on show everywhere. Yet, as that image of the young Thembu aristocrat with the steam-iron in his hand suggests, while this glamour may have appeared to him as the quintessential expression of the urban world, it was not entirely new. In the Transkei his guardian had used the material privileges that accrued to his position to acquire the appurtenances of the modern African: not only the dress and car, but also the western-style houses and university-educated advisors.

However, for the Christianized Chief Jongintaba, as for his relative Mandela, modernity was from the beginning to be defined not merely through material display, but through an ability to deploy different social registers and roles in relation to different audiences. For both men, 'tradition' was never a simple inheritance from the past, but was understood as bound up with the modern present in complicated ways. The jagged, diverse effects of modernity offered both powerful modes of resistance to the ways in which the apartheid system repressed Africans by retribalizing them, homogenizing them as 'native' and 'primitive'.

Some biographical accounts of Mandela in the 1940s and 1950s suggest that he assumed an observer status relative to the teeming spectacle of the African city. Yet, looking more closely at where he socialized and how he dressed in these years, it becomes apparent that he thrived in the scene, as an active if temperate participant. Indeed, some regarded him as insufficiently serious to be a politician. A teetotaller, he did not frequent the *shebeens*, yet he frequently ate in downtown restaurants like the Blue Lagoon and the Mauritian-owned Indian restaurant Kapitan's in Kort Street, where he developed a strong and lasting liking for prawn curry (see Figure 10 in the last chapter). From these vantage points he watched the passing display of well-heeled African fashion: *tsotsis* sporting Woodrow hats and Hagar slacks, cruising the streets in long, finned American cars.

A memorable image of Mandela at this time—'a tall, handsome man with hair parted in the middle...wearing a charcoal grey suit and [flashing] a big white-toothed smile of success' (etched in Lewis Nkosi's *Mandela's Ego*)—rightly evokes an individual solicitous of his appearance, a follower of fashion (Figure 12). It is well-known that throughout his career, even during prison visits, Mandela made a point of looking groomed. He adored women's

12. Rolihlahla Nelson Mandela in the early 1950s, at this point already known for his formal elegance and style.

attention and, though married, probably had several lovers. When arrested in 1956, his strongest impression was of the relative physical unfitness of his fellow inmates. Few had 'the symmetrical build of Shaka', he observed. This was undoubtedly someone not displeased with his own commanding physical stature (1.90 metres tall), aware that such height showed off a tailored suit to good advantage. Fellow ANC campaigner Ellen Kuzwayo always remembered Nelson as the 'glamorous one' among the *troika* he formed with Walter and Oliver.

> I remember the glamorous Nelson Mandela of those years.
>
> The beautiful white silk scarf he wore around his neck stands out in my mind to this day. Walter Max Sisulu, on the other hand, was a hardy, down-to-earth man with practical clothing—typically a heavy coat and stout boots. Looking back, the third member of their trio, Oliver Tambo, acted as something of a balance, with his middle-of-the-road clothes!
>
> Ellen Kuzwayo, from *Call Me Woman* (1985)

Mandela's Johannesburg years were, from the start, extremely busy, taken up first with study and legal work, and later, increasingly, with political activity, even during his banned periods. The waiting room at the Tambo and Mandela law offices was usually full to bursting. Yet, while carrying out his duties as an attorney, he kept in mind the social and political importance for not only a black professional but also a politician of *looking the part*, of representing the modernity and confidence to which people aspired, of expressing urban possibility. Although the ANC was relatively uninterested in debates about cultural politics, and the Sophiatown writers were, with equal but opposite force, dismissive of politicized art, ANC rallies in Sophiatown's Freedom Square juxtaposed style and politics, activism and art, in provocative, eye-catching ways that would have impressed the image-conscious Nelson.

Tellingly, Mandela was known to be on first-name terms with many of the Johannesburg gang-leaders, such as Kortboy of the Americans. And how could he not, when ANC meetings were held in venues like the Moretsele Hotel, where the Americans went to have breakfast? He was conversant in the local patois, a 'broken' mix of Afrikaans, Zulu, and Chicago-ese called *tsotsitaal* (English being deemed highfalutin). The many photographs of Mandela dating from this period, especially studio pictures by Eli Weinberg and Peter Magubane, pay flamboyant testimony to the many roles he played and the different costumes he donned to play them. As well as the lawyer formally posed in his office with a vase of agapanthus, the photographs show the bridegroom, the Thembu chief, the public speaker, the activist, the boxer (Figure 12). Besides the cut of his suits, striking details include the patterned (including floral) ties he wore—decades before these became fashionable among young professionals.

But perhaps the most telling evidence of Mandela's intensive urban involvement was his passion for boxing, for which he trained for ninety minutes a day at an Orlando gym (Figure 11). Boxing was not merely the black majority's number-one sport, drawing vast and varied audiences; it was also an activity demanding excellent physical form, individualism, strategy, and, above all, showmanship. It suited Mandela in every respect. Another reconstructed reminiscence of this time, Njabulo Ndebele's redemptive evocation *The Cry of Winnie Mandela*, reminds us that Nelson 'used to have [Winnie] picked up so [she] could watch him at the gym, or at meetings, or at rallies. How charming!...[They were] part of the glitz of Orlando, Sophiatown, Thulandiville, the entire network of reef townships.'

He was a peacock showing off his feathers to a potential mating partner. So handsome. And you, so stunningly beautiful. The glamour of celebrity and the danger of politics came together in an elaborate foreplay of social energy.

Njabulo Ndebele, from *The Cry of Winnie Mandela* (2003)

Drum magazine: Sophiatown's voice

The most memorable record of the 'fabulous decade', as Lewis
Nkosi dubbed it, was imprinted in *Drum* magazine, a tabloid-style
paper for Africans established in 1951. It was in these pages that
the Sophiatown generation of 'de-tribalized African cockneys'
found its voice. Though edited and owned by whites, *Drum* made
the careers of a host of talented writers including the exposé
journalist Henry Nxumalo ('Mr Drum'), Nat Nakasa, Bloke
Modisane, Can Themba, Nkosi himself. On its showbiz pages as in
its reportage, in its sports journalism as in its stylish short stories,
the *Drum* writers captured the characteristic tone of Sophiatown,
a vigorous, slangy 'jazz speak'.

Appealing to a continental, Pan-African readership, *Drum*
communicated both at a higher-brow, literary level and, more
usually, through a semi-literate picture language featuring
beauty queens, boxers, social workers, respectable family
patriarchs—pictures that represented role models for the target
black bourgeois audience. Significantly, Nelson and Winnie
Mandela taken together as a couple embodied some of the most
prominent of these roles. Mandela, pictured in a good suit at the
Treason Trial, was a 1956 *Drum* 'cover boy'. His showcasing as
the archetypal African cosmopolitan and bespoke nationalist
politician is therefore to a degree attributable to the efforts of
the talented *Drum* generation of writers. From the standpoint
of this literary community, as aware of the importance of
self-presentation as of self-representation, of black style as of
black pride, the smart politician with the film-star smile appeared
as a definitive leader in so far as he was *also* an unparalleled
urban sophisticate.

Reflecting on the historical moment of *Drum*, the writer Ezekiel
Mphahlehle once said: we '[dig] our feet into an urban culture on
impossible terms...Ours is a fugitive culture: borrowing here,

incorporating there, retaining this, rejecting that.' Tragically, it was also a fugitive culture in that, by the mid-1960s, with Johannesburg's 'black spot' removals long completed, its most prominent players were on the run, in gaol, or in exile. Marlene van Niekerk's gutting novel *Triomf* (1994) refracts the dysfunctional white working-class suburb built on Kofifi's ruins. Today, the sad demise of the fabulous *Drum* generation of artists polishes its glamorous image by contrast, and gives the 1950s Mandela, the man about Sophiatown, the air of a figure from a distant age. Yet the concept of an impossible, fugitive black culture is important, too, for what it says about the symbolic struggle that urban life represented for self-consciously modern Africans. Like the lawyers Tambo and Mandela, like the *shebeen* trumpeters and crooners, *Drum*'s writers worked with a live sense of creating against the odds conditions of self-determination for black city-dwellers.

* * *

Apartheid was not merely an institutional order but a 'predicament' (Leon de Kock), which meant that for urban Africans to enter official history, they had willy-nilly to commit a kind of torsion upon it. Recasting European forms in their own terms, they forged a 'suture of the incommensurate'. With its stories of desperate battles for survival and transient moments of romance before inevitable loss, *Drum* magazine's pages outline how tough it was for black South Africans to make this historical entry and live this fissured reality, and, moreover, to do so with grace and style. *Drum* shows what feats of adaptation and ingenuity were required to map a coherent and above all modish path through the apartheid condition, whether via political resistance like Sophiatown's 'We Won't Move' campaign, or in writing itself.

During the years Mandela spent working in the intercultural hurly-burly of central Johannesburg, he developed the dynamism (the quality Sisulu first discerned in him) that allowed him to override the feelings of self-alienation that bruised many of his peers, and to burst into the modern present. As much as from

Gandhi's by-1952-historically-distant example, he learned from the spectacle of Sophiatown to choreograph an image in order to press a political point. In the downtown streets where the flashy personality was encouraged to present the star turn that was himself, he honed the showman-like confidence that he would use to great public effect at Rivonia, to give one of the 20th century's great speeches, and, much later, within the lower key forum of the negotiation table. As we will see next, he here perceived that an assured masculine style could effectively counter the prevailing stereotypes of black people as backward, rural, and the like. Indeed, he had by 1962 become so advanced as an agent of history, a self-conscious political operator within and between communities, that he liked to phone journalists to report on his own movements underground.

Mandela's capacity for self-projection despite apartheid repression is explored in the next chapter, which foregrounds the ANC leader as a turbo-charged, intensely masculine performer. Yet not only his mask-wearing and shape-shifting, but also, a related quality, his relative freedom from dogma, can be explained by the fact that his political education took place within the crucible of South African jazz. Only with difficulty could his sensibilities have escaped the atmosphere of risk and improvisation, of extravagant borrowing and freewheeling style that characterized Johannesburg's mixed dance halls and music clubs. His political practice ever since, it can be argued, was noticeably marked by the rhythms and syncopations of Fordsburg and Sophiatown's music, its contrapuntal interminglings, blues notes, and offbeat tangents. Throughout his career, he often interested himself in pursuing an *experimental line* (in novelist J. M. Coetzee's phrase) in contradistinction to his party's line. He showed the critical courage of the jazzman, as Cornel West writes. He advocated violence when other ANC leaders stuck to passive resistance. In prison he built a rapport with the enemy. And, even if the response was belated, he promoted HIV/AIDS awareness when the South African state policy was to deny the existence of AIDS.

Chapter 6
Masculine performer

At his trials in both 1962 and 1964, Mandela chose, after consultation, to represent himself in the dock, thinking that the direct form of address this afforded him would create an ideal opportunity for broadcasting the political vision of the already-banned ANC. In this he was massively successful. His two strategically planned and rhetorically patterned speeches propelled the African nationalists' anti-apartheid fight onto the world stage, and, moreover, shone the historical limelight centrally on Mandela.

In any memoir involving the ANC leader, this is the keynote that is repeatedly struck: his chameleon-like talent for donning different guises; his theatrical flair for costume and gesture; his shrewd awareness of audience and the power of his own image. Across his career he played such varied roles as counsellor, lawyer, showman, guerrilla leader, and statesman, and allowed himself to be profligately photographed in these guises. As we saw, he delighted in acting the *shape-shifter*, assuming a range of contrasting masks and mien, and convincing others of their authenticity. His city persona, for example, expressed a contemporary yet unmistakably African nationalist self-assurance: *this*, his look proclaimed, was the style of the coming African man, the citizen of the future.

On the run in 1961–2, he positively thrived in the outfits his life-in-hiding necessitated, and in the sense of theatre and risk of exposure involved in wearing them (see Figure 9). Not for nothing was he called the Black Pimpernel, after the protagonist of Baroness Orczy's then-popular 1905 novel *The Scarlet Pimpernel* about an aristocratic English master of ingenious disguises working at the time of the French Terror. Mandela is said not to have resented the appellation. It appealed to his sense of himself as able to establish rapport with a variety of different audiences—'with Muslims in the Cape . . . sugar-workers in Natal . . . factory workers in Port Elizabeth', he wrote in his autobiography. It appealed also to his desire for mastery of any situation in which he might find himself: a feature that *Long Walk to Freedom* does not, by contrast, openly address.

This chapter highlights Nelson Mandela's breathtaking abilities as a performer and manipulator of images—qualities central to an understanding of his historical achievement, and of how this intersected with the ANC's political vision. From the late 1950s, especially after the controversial shift to violence, it is clear that his organization, despite its emphasis on the collective, tirelessly worked to exploit his self-projection as a symbolic man-of-destiny. For an exiled movement in need of messianic leadership, Mandela fitted the bill perfectly and, indeed, was happy so to style his image.

It is this that underpins the choreographed quality to which any account of his life inevitably testifies: his performances were composed with a remarkable degree of self-knowledge. He was never unaware of the power of making a physical statement; of the efficacy, whether in public or private, of masks; of how his life might be read as a model for African upward mobility and political success. Even on the 1994 campaign trail, when his reputation was relatively secure, he was famous for addressing a number of People's Forums in one day, changing several times to suit his different audiences (a woolly jumper for a talk to older people; an open shirt for a village crowd). As Mhlaba once remarked, Mandela from the late 1950s was groomed to be the internal ANC leader (the counterpart to Tambo in exile): 'he himself of course conducted himself to attain that status'.

Mandela's mastery of performance, taken as a given during his life, remains worth analysing in depth even so many years after his death. In part, it is important to confront the occasional association of such theatricality with charges of changeability and moral hollowness. Yet his capacity for working his image as if it were itself an expression of his politics also tells us a great deal about his shrewd ability to manipulate his own myth. It reflects on his proverbial dynamism, how he transformed his *style of activism* into a *credo for action*. And it relays his understanding, which he shared with Gandhi, that method and medium are central to politics; that principle is most effectively conveyed through display. Political success to a great extent means transmitting a more humanly convincing message than does one's rival: Mandela keenly embraced this precept. This alone gives reason to examine his capacity as a consummate player of roles.

Mandela's awareness of his iconic status can appear cynical, even occasionally craven, especially later in life, when, as his assistant Zelda La Grange observed, he sometimes actively courted public attention. However, for his time, this awareness is most accurately described as expedient. He saw, as did Nehru, that it was important to stand as a 'symbolic expression of the confused desires of his people': that embattled anti-colonial nationalist movements required compelling, unifying images. A reader of Nehru's life-writing, Mandela in his own autobiography fifty years later constructed his life on the assumption that the leader's story is interlocked with the nation's—specifically, for him, the story of anti-apartheid resistance. In his view, the leader, the first democratic president-to-be, embodied the nation. Significantly, during his later years in office, Mandela often presented in ways that suggested a self entirely bound up in a public mask, as his co-biographer Richard Stengel commented.

Another strong reason for an analysis of the performer-president is that Mandela in role—*unlike* that other arch-performer, Gandhi—tended to act the man, in ways that reinforced or enhanced his masculinity. If his iconography to some extent emblematized his politics, it was a noticeably masculine iconography. To speak of Mandela the man of masks, therefore, requires us to speak also of his projection of a consistently masterful masculinity, though seasoned, especially in later years, with sensitivity and feeling. His 'affective dynamism' became a commanding way of presenting himself in the public sphere. Due to the widespread preconception, at least at the time, that a national leader had necessarily to be assertive, a predominant masculinity is often assumed in studies of Mandela, as is his persona of ladies' man. However, it also provided, certainly in the first half of his career, the motor force behind his political authority and moral conduct.

Sartorial display

When he entered court for the first time after his high-profile 1962 arrest, Mandela famously wore traditional Xhosa dress, a leopard-skin *kaross*, or robe, with beads around his neck and legs. Selected by Winnie to complement her own Mpondoland headdress and skirt, the outfit demonstrated that he was carrying on his shoulders his people's historical aspirations. 'I felt myself to be the embodiment of African nationalism', he commented. At other times, as we know, he donned smart lawyer's suits to radiate urbanity—suits that were likewise matched by Winnie's sophisticated, modern style (Figure 13). His liking for the 'trappings of British style and manners' refracted his respect for Westminster democracy and gentlemanly values.

13. Mandela celebrates outside court with his wife Winnie after his acquittal at the end of the Treason Trial. Already sporting the beard of the elusive 'Black Pimpernel', he would that very night begin his life underground. The photograph conveys the couple's performative intimacy, the memory of which sustained him during the long years in prison.

Later, taking the part of Creon in the 1970 Robben Island production of Sophocles' *Antigone*, Mandela said he experienced what it was to be a true law-maker: the role and the robes gave the feeling of reality. By the time of his presidency, his public character seemed to have become one with the infectious smile and bonhomie he had long cultivated. His interactions with the media were almost entirely constituted through the medium of charm, which most were helpless to resist. He artfully combined freedom-fighter celebrity with middle-class respectability, as when he controversially drank tea with Mrs Verwoerd. He had achieved what one of his cabinet ministers described as a total politicization of being.

The predominant aspect of the many eye-catching performances that distinguish Mandela's career is this strong emphasis on sartorial display: not only acting the part, but also donning the right costume. As for that other political magus of semiotics, Gandhi, clothing and style were central to how Mandela projected himself. He worked the vocabulary of dress to assert his control over a situation and to encapsulate the values he espoused. By contrast, his speeches were often unremarkable, characterized by an overuse of set-piece motifs and struggle rhetoric, a fondness for cliché (such as human life being but a brief flash upon a stage), and an admonishing tone (at times not unlike that of his white counterpart, P. W. Botha).

Mandela's heavy-handed rhetorical formality connected also to the relative invisibility of the physical and emotive body in his speeches—though so present in his sensually charged prison letters to Winnie. In contradistinction to his imposing stature, matters concerning bodily involvement, including sexuality or any form of kinaesthetic, are curiously recessive or expressed only with extreme modesty. This is an area of noticeable difference from Gandhi, who was unstinting in the projection of his semi-attired, physical (if ascetic) body to better signify his politics of self-restraint.

In Mandela's case, therefore, clothes most definitely made the man and the politician. Dress transmitted the moral example—and the model of style—which he sought to represent on almost every platform he occupied. For him, the most significant political moments were captured in some appropriate costume, to the extent that in certain instances, as in his wearing the traditional green-and-gold Springbok rugby shirt and cap at South Africa's 1995 World Cup victory, the costume *created* the moment (Figure 14). On that July day, he knowingly played both with the standard signifiers of white South African masculinity and with the elasticity of his own media image. Far from baulking at the cringe-worthy commonplaces with which the event was loaded, as J. M. Coetzee once remarked, Mandela embraced them, assisted in this by the Springbok captain's known political sensitivity. Though the performance appeared compromising to some observers, he sought to embody thereby the principle of reconciliation with Afrikanerdom, as the 2009 film *Invictus* reflects.

In maverick ways unnervingly similar to those of imperial heroes like Robert Baden-Powell or indeed Lord Nelson himself—who might also have taken Henley's 'Invictus' as their inspiration— Mandela revelled in a sense of public occasion, the combination of formality and drama, convention and improvisation. He enjoyed mastering a situation through sheer verve, guts, and willpower. He also demonstrated a strong sense of historical destiny, understanding that the conviction of being appointed to a task, coupled with an aptitude for theatricality, was central to authoritative leadership. If in later years, as he ever more closely approximated his own myth as secular saint, he sacrificed the trickster qualities of his previous incarnations—the young joker, the Pimpernel-on-the-run—his costumes continued to remind audiences of his wayward humour and untiring pleasure in striking a pose.

Nelson Mandela

14. Mandela enters sporting legend by wearing captain François Pienaar's No. 6 rugby shirt at the Springboks' 1995 Rugby World Cup victory.

Embodiment of the law

From the time of his entry onto a wider political stage with the Defiance Campaign, Mandela was aware that a leader's political prospectus should encapsulate his people's aspirations, and that his physical presence in performance could be seen to configure the nation's dreams. In his law practice with Tambo, established that same year, Mandela quickly built a reputation as an assertive advocate, cultivating a theatrical manner in court which contrasted with his partner's more retiring approach. He saw that his profession as a black lawyer working amid the contradictions of apartheid society demanded this dramatic boldness—indispensable armour in a context where black people were routinely humiliated.

But his performances also shrewdly invoked the values that underlay his professional success: the patrimonial loyalties to community reinforced by the Victorian principle of self-help; the etiquette instilled by his mission education; his respect for reasoned debate and the rule of law. *See!* his court appearances announced, here is a black man outdoing the white at representing the very civilized values that he, the white man, would deny me. The impact was supremely subversive, precisely because, in making his claims, Mandela was incarnating the principles of law and liberty that white authority attached exclusively to itself.

By the time of his 1962 trial for sabotage, Mandela was more aware than most that the space of the court could be used as a political theatre. It was a place unconstrained like no other in the country by the discriminatory restrictions imposed on Africans. His 1964 speech from the dock, with its step-by-step exposition of the ANC's history and its turn to armed violence, also demonstrated this awareness of historical moment and audience, and of the sheer freedom that the opportunity to expound afforded.

Throughout the speech, Mandela carefully balanced his different allegiances—to tradition and modernity, to nationalism and communism, to the west and Africa. He was conscious that each measured word delivered an exposé of the injustices black South Africans had suffered, *and*, even more powerfully, dramatized the black commitment to justice in contrast with the 'banditry' of white law (in Bloke Modisane's memorable phrase). He gave authoritative witness to black integrity and capability here, now, within South Africa. In a 1986 essay, the French philosopher Jacques Derrida memorably analysed Mandela's invocation of the pure spirit of the law. Appealing over the heads of his judges, representatives of a debased law, Derrida wrote, Mandela stood for a higher justice. '[Setting] himself against the code within the code', he became the ultimate expression of the rationalist legal traditions associated with the Enlightenment.

In prison, deprived of the underpinnings of authority provided by the public stage and appropriate dress, Mandela developed other methods of asserting his vision and will, which again, however, involved self-projection, if in more intimate surroundings. It was entirely predictable that the first complaint he lodged targeted the demeaning short trousers African prisoners were forced to wear. At issue, yet again, was the way in which dress configured personal and political dignity. In the confined corners of cell and exercise yard, he also explored the possibilities for a different type of discourse. The fiery guerrilla leader modulated perforce into the low-profile interlocutor who, with his eye still on the look of any action, often singled out individuals from other organizations for conversation. In his interactions with the prison authorities he always remained impeccably correct in his manners, even when provoked. Visitors, announced or unexpected, he addressed with characteristic gravity. Politeness was again a way of demonstrating, through contrast, African self-mastery and respect for the law.

Following his 1990 release, when his image once again went public, then, too, Mandela the man worked together with the myth his organization had built, to communicate representativeness, in particular. He vigorously rejected any notion of occupying an elevated position, and spoke of the danger of personality cults in African politics. Yet his brokering between the ANC and the government depended precisely on the authority he bore as an individual leader, his capacity to *speak for* his movement and country, and *to* his people, as his famously liberal use of the collective first person suggested. The many times on which he sued for compromise depended almost entirely on this store of moral capital, of acting in ways consistent with his core principles. On the hustings in 1994, he fully identified himself with his organization's campaign. He signified in his practice and upon his body the prestige he had acquired as a young commander and political prisoner, but also, even more intensively, he encapsulated a prospective new South African identity—liberated, expansive, mobile, inclusive.

It was predictable that this national message would, yet again, be expressed sartorially. In the early to mid-1990s, Mandela took to wearing the relaxed, colourful Madiba shirts that became his trademark—and a desirable commodity in South African tourist shops (see Figures 9 and 20). Indonesian President Suharto had introduced Mandela to these shirts on his 1990 Asian tour; they were far from being authentically African. He adopted the loose-fitting but dressy garment not so much for how it harmonized with the concept of the rainbow nation, as might appear, but because of its comfort. Yet, while allowing him to 'feel freedom' (his words), the shirt also permitted him to configure an old man's hard-won but still dignified casualness, with ethnic rainbow hues thrown into the mix.

In short, from as far back as 1952, certainly in the years 1990–9, Mandela's political life can be viewed as an ongoing publicity event, in which he was both the centrepiece and the most relentless of managers. In a conflict with unpredictable adversaries, he keenly perceived, the constant retooling of image was crucial. In the 2000s, his smiling face ubiquitously featured on South African tourist industry websites. To this day, the name Mandela remains synonymous with that of his country.

Formal speech

No account of Mandela the showman is complete without giving attention to the curious plainness of his verbal performances: the affect-less tone that marked his early speeches continued, though with some modification, to run as a mode across his career. This stiffness also characterized his polemical articles written for publications like *Liberation* (1953–9), and his political-pedagogical statements in prison. How did this *langue de bois*, in Achille Mbembe's phrase, coordinate with the versatility of his statesman-like behaviour?

Rhetoric, according to the classic definition, is fundamental to persuasion, just as good delivery is to a successful performance. For Mandela, however, persuasion often depended rather on the projection of leaderly authority through correct and even mechanical forms of address. In 'Tamed', written in response to the February 1990 'Release' speech, the poet Tatamkhulu Afrika suggestively describes Mandela as both a godhead, raised on an 'alienating pedestal, piled for your pinioning', and a mere old man, manipulated by historical forces, fed 'stolidly' with words 'as into a machine'. Across the years, as this implies, Mandela's sartorial language often worked with more eloquent effect than his formal speeches, though his verbal stolidity at the same time underpinned his chiefly demeanour.

Rather than being a master of post-apartheid rhetoric, as the critic Philippe-Joseph Salazar suggests, Mandela could instead be said to have deployed the *rhetoric of post-apartheid mastery*. This is apparent from that same 11 February speech, drafted together with Cyril Ramaphosa and Trevor Manuel. At this time of the re-emergence of the leader-in-waiting, the concern of the speech-writing *troika* was to assert collective leadership and dispel suspicions regarding any possible collaboration with the enemy. Hence, much to the disappointment of some listeners, Mandela's adherence throughout to longwinded, formal, and formulaic salutations to the ANC's supporting constituencies. Similar litanies of acknowledgement marked other speeches at the time. (Interestingly, although Mandela worked with several different speech-writers during his career, this quality of his language remained a constant and so, presumably, a preference.)

It is indicative that Mandela was always a more impressive speaker in court than out of it. The lawyer's bench and the dock granted him a certain licence, where he learned to modulate his tone to fit the contours of a legal argument. Elsewhere, motivated by a strong sense of responsibility to his people, he consistently avoided appearing the demagogue. To encourage support, he used a pared-down, generalist language, the verbs straightforward and workmanlike, the nouns often abstract—invoking freedom, democracy—but unadorned. In all cases, in the dock and on the podium, his reasoned stage-by-stage progressions and set phrases were designed to control the expression of subjective emotion.

Except on those relatively rare occasions when his anger at an abuse of power was expressed as exhortation, Mandela's was a public discourse from which the affect had been extracted. We were not to know how Madiba felt, how Rolihlahla felt. For one as dedicated as he was to achieving consensus through the assertion of agreed-upon principles, it made no sense to amplify or overqualify his words. His repetitive, starkly polarized binaries (dark/light, life/death, African people/white government); the predictable imagery of extensive battles, long walks, and slow upward climbs (made safe by endorsements from Shakespeare and Nehru)—in short, the clichés he so preferred were first and foremost a means of insisting upon concord.

The tension that exists in Mandela between two modes of leadership, in biographer Tom Lodge's reading, is stamped on these verbal performances. It lies in the contrast between the occasional roused, magisterial tones, on the one hand, and the more deadpan, ministerial delivery, on the other. Inspired by his courtly background, he at times subscribed to traditional notions of consensual decision-making. This approach was arguably expressed via an authoritative vocabulary of collective identification and occasional reliance on embellishment and mini-allegory, as in his well-known citation of the Ingrid Jonker poem (about the African child bestriding the world) in the 24 May 1994 State of the Nation address. Elsewhere, however, he used the tried-and-tested formulae of liberal self-determination and democratic rule. He revealingly deployed this same telegraphic, empirical language, pitted against the excesses of the colonial state, in his 1960s justifications of armed resistance. It was this second mode, too, that—to close a circle—provided the strategic foil to his exuberant, individualized performances on the political stage.

Masculine Madiba

From the time he entered his guardian-the-regent's court, through his legal and political work in Johannesburg, to the prison years, each one of the social-cultural worlds Mandela occupied was organized on patriarchal lines underpinned by masculinist values. Small wonder then that across most of his life he viewed not merely national heroism but historical agency itself in masculine terms. Small wonder, too, that in his supporters' eyes, his assertive, heterosexual masculinity represented the taken-for-granted scaffolding for his charismatic leadership.

In his 1964 court notes made in the event that a death sentence was pronounced, Mandela's pride in his cause was resonantly expressed in the final words, that he would go to meet his fate 'like a man' (see Figure 4). The words echoed the cry the initiate

Rolihlahla had battled to utter at the moment of his circumcision. As for most postcolonial nationalist movements up to that point, to be a human subject for Mandela was to be a man. In his autobiography, though published in 1994, the South African liberation struggle is generically described as the 'black man's' experience. For Mandela, nationalist self-assertion involved fully coming into one's own as a man—this despite his hospitality to women's modes of protest.

Under empire, as is now widely recognized, gender identities were enlisted in the service of colonial power. Within the colonial hierarchy, European authority tended to be cast as masculine (dominant, rational), while social regulations and cultural representations effeminized the colonized, in particular the men, to better effect their subjugation. Significantly, in several letters of complaint written in prison, Mandela referred to the abuses the inmates suffered as emasculating. In South Africa, the 1910 white union had substantially reinforced the discriminatory colonial regime of masculine and feminine value that had operated from the 1700s. Its draconian land and labour laws polarized families along strict gender lines, eventually penning migrant mineworkers in all-male compounds in the cities.

As in other former colonies, therefore, in South Africa the subversion of imposed gender ideologies became a fundamental anti-colonial strategy. Prominent figures in the nationalist community felt bound to assert a forceful, overcompensatory masculinity, counterpointed by the elevation of rural mothers as symbols of national virtue. Moreover, in a context in which both mission school and workplace reproduced the traditional family's patriarchal framework, the story of the African's entry into urban modernity became, almost inevitably, a male-dominated story. Although Mandela grew up at a remove from direct colonialism, his Johannesburg worlds were at once colonial and patriarchal in their divisions. Here, both black nationalists and urban sophisticates resisted discrimination through representing as 'manly' men. The projection of a *hyper-masculinity*, in theorist Ashis Nandy's memorable phrase—a masculinity that was aggressive, uncompromising, domineering towards women—was the stance that the male African nationalist was under pressure to adopt. This same attitude expressed in the fantasy of the struggle couple was often projected on Nelson Mandela and Winnie Madikizela-Mandela in the 1990s: he the imposing father of the nation, she the Mother fallen from grace, as Brenna Munro writes.

Mandela is on record for having said that it wasn't till the time for reflection his prison years afforded that he began to develop a more critical attitude towards the conventional equation of leadership with masculinity. At the Great Place the young Nelson had, after all, witnessed Jongintaba's authoritarian rule expressed as deliberation exclusively between male chiefs. The 'home boy' networks he used to get ahead in Johannesburg played to the advantage of those who stood upon their traditional status. As in Can Themba's *Drum* story 'Mob Passion', the cultural spaces of the city—the Bantu Men's Social Club, jazz clubs, the magazine's pages itself—constituted macho worlds where he found he could thrive precisely by burnishing his easygoing but dynamic masculine persona.

True, as someone impressed by the 'intelligent' women students at Fort Hare, Mandela sought out, as his first and second wives, women who were educated professionals. He recognized that their success represented a significant achievement for black women at the time. Even so, as his biographers relate, his relationships with Evelyn and Winnie were characterized by conventional gender expectations around decision-making, agency, and fidelity. He presented Evelyn Mase with their divorce papers as a *fait accompli*. His courtship of Winnie Madikizela, conducted while he was involved in the Treason Trial, was often stage-managed by him: his proposal came in the form of an announcement that her wedding dress had been ordered. (Her own ideas about her power and agency in the matter would prove to be very different.)

x

Nelson Mandela

For him, as in *Drum*, urban modernity meant conformity to the ideals of bourgeois domesticity. On Robben Island, in 1970, he finally wrote to Winnie to convey regret at having left her to child-rearing without more considerate help from him.

In the political realm, too, in contradistinction to how African men in white service were addressed as 'boys', the ANC, and its Youth League in particular, expressed nationalist aspiration via images of combativeness and virility, while threats to the same, conversely, were seen as affronts to masculinity. Lilian Ngoyi, ANC Women's League president in the 1950s, a lover of Mandela's at the time of the breakup of his first marriage, was interestingly represented in *Drum* as a fearsome ball-breaker and, at the same time, as soft inside, confirming gender dichotomies. Mandela himself, self-reliant from an early age, comfortable with the gravitas of status, used to assuming a masterly air, was able to project an overtly masculine persona relatively effortlessly, if also self-consciously. In his aggressive heckling at meetings, as in his gentlemanly court demeanour, he conducted himself so as to reinforce an indubitable African authority.

His assured role-play was also prominently on show in his relaxed friendships with white women like Helen Joseph, Ruth First, and Mary Benson associated with the Congress of Democrats and the ANC—friendships that his male biographers describe as remarkable (though they were all *haute-bourgeois* ladies). In many anti-colonial contexts, it has been the case that the nationalist hero's masculinity is heightened through his connection with an allegedly prized white femininity. Such connection represented not merely the desire for the sexually forbidden—the more obvious explanation—but a yearning for less uneven gender relations than were generally possible with black women, given colonial hierarchies. For Mandela, it is clear, these friendships were fuelled by an intellectual pleasure in meeting with women, of whatever race, on an equal footing as fellow activists. With Helen Joseph (Figure 15), for example, he felt sufficiently at ease to talk

My dear Helen,

Your last letter had the same effect on me & Maki. It scratched the feelings of kinship which your frequent letters to us since she was admitted to S.H. In one of the latest letters to me she spoke for both of us when she said: "I am happy and relieved now. Aunt Helen wrote me a letter and she usually phones."

Of course I was confident from the outset that once you receive my letter you would literally ransack the whole country to help the young lady through her problems. My real worry was due to the fact that experience has made correspondence an unreliable method of communication, even though correspondence between you & me has so far proceeded smoothly. I was also certain that in handling the matter, you would do more than respond to the specific request I made. Your last letter fully justified that confidence.

15. A typically comradely letter from Robben Island to Helen Joseph, dated 13 May 1979, in which Mandela asks her to assist with minding his daughter Maki's affairs, and talks about religion, and missing his friends. People like Joseph represented an indispensable lifeline during the long prison years, which, despite many disruptions, helped Mandela's wife and daughters to maintain a rudimentary day-to-day existence as a family.

about his initiation while *en route* to the Treason Trial in her car. He forged lasting contacts, too, with the wives of his Indian Congress colleagues, like Amina Cachalia, who inducted him into the pleasures of their cooking. In his autobiography he discusses gravitating towards women, as with them he could 'confess to weaknesses and fears I could never reveal to another man': he felt free to act as less dominantly masculine. In their turn, these women, without exception, felt charmed by his politeness, cordiality, and impressive physique.

Yet if Mandela's masculinist, heterosexual role-play consistently formed an expression of his politics, it was not engaged without tension, as was brought out by his thoughtful, eclectic reading in prison. One of the first women writers he ever encountered, his 'precious girl' Nadine Gordimer, especially her *Burger's Daughter*, took him 'beyond visible horizons', he once commented, and changed his perspective on gender roles in the struggle. Whereas Winnie had long chafed at his conventionality, he now began to write to her in ways that better acknowledged their partnership: 'with you on my side' he said in 1969, 'I always feel part of an invincible force that is ready to win new worlds'. Many of his early attitudes towards women had been 'totally wrong'. He expressed admiration for figures like Margaret Thatcher (her political determination as a woman prime minister, not her politics), and for powerful widows in his own Thembuland lineage.

Mandela's raised gender awareness was confirmed in his partnership with his third wife, Graça Machel. The widow of Samora Machel had been for some considerable time an important feminist and public figure in her own right in her native Mozambique. With her marriage to Mandela she arguably extended these roles. Even so, distance from his former masculinist preconceptions did not diminish his delight in posing alongside the range of media and fashion beauties he entertained in his post-prison years (Princess Diana, the Spice Girls, Oprah

Winfrey, Charlize Theron) (see Figure 8). Yet his charmed collusion in the media objectification of these women is arguably tempered by his willingness to stand alongside them as a pin-up, and, more generally, to offer himself as a figurehead for various causes: the HIV/AIDS awareness campaign; his own Children's Fund.

Mandela's robust masculinity always assumed a largely unexamined heterosexuality as its foundation, though here again there are points of ambivalence. In prison he appears to have overlooked homosexual occurrences, on the grounds first of alleged ignorance, and, once disabused of this, of disgust, though he was willing to admit in principle that such 'unnatural' acts might take place. Years later, however, when he belatedly espoused the HIV/AIDS campaign, he made the controversial acknowledgement that this 'Western' 'gay disease' had become an African disease also: it was important, he felt, to 'break the silence'. In prison, too, though he maintained his own silence about his feelings, Mandela was never afraid to show tenderness and solicitousness towards his friends. This quality emerged especially in his relations with short-statured Eddie Daniels, the member of the Liberal Party's militant offshoot ARM who at times felt marginalized within the Island's 'B Section'. Mandela taught Daniels the to-him-heartening lines of 'Invictus', and personally assisted him by emptying his chamber pot when he was ill. Occasionally he revealed to Daniels the emotional pain imposed by his own regime of self-control.

Neolitha's body

I have been fairly successful in putting on a mask behind which I have pined for the family, alone, never rushing for the post when it comes until somebody calls out my name. I also never linger after visits although sometimes the urge to do so becomes quite terrible. I am struggling to suppress my emotions as I write this letter. I have received only one letter since you were detained, that one dated August 22. I do not know anything about family affairs, such as payment of rent, telephone bills, care of children and their expenses, whether you will get a job when released. As long as I don't hear from you, I will remain worried and dry like a desert. I recall the Karoo I crossed on several occasions. I saw the desert again in Botswana on my way to and from Africa—endless pits of sand and not a drop of water. I have not had a letter from you. I feel dry like the desert. Letters from you and the family are like the arrival of summer rains and spring that liven my life and make it enjoyable. Whenever I write to you I feel that inside physical warmth, that makes me forget all my problems. I become full of love.

Nelson Mandela, from a letter to Winnie Mandela (October 1976)

The contusion in Mandela of exuberant performance and suppressed feeling points to the possibility that his dazzling masculine act, including as a debonair president receiving celebrities, itself involved studied sensory management. Did his Teflon masculinity constitute one of the primary defences making up his protective social shield? His appearances with female icons from the worlds of entertainment and charity showbiz featured theatrical flattery and scripted lines—acts which became ever more repetitive and superficial the more the president spoke of himself in private as the 'loneliest man'. Was his masculine role-play, as this suggests, caught up in the masks he was so good at maintaining, rather than with the feeling human being? And might the self-control, to which this successful masculine front was bolted, connect with that remarkable absence of the corporeal body from his public speeches, even his talks about HIV/AIDS?

The child who from an early age learned to exercise extreme self-discipline, Mandela always exhibited an 'aversion to personal discussion'. Expressions of vulnerability he confined to letters, as in his October 1976 letter to Winnie about wearing protective masks (above). Emotional crises, whether of desire or sorrow, were always contained: indeed, his mask appeared to emerge from his negation of his potentially weak, 'feminine' body. To Mandela, the body was altogether too chaotic an entity to admit into the masculine domain of nationalist politics, even when this was limited to the prison yard.

[I]n the quietness of the day's dawning, [Mandela] told another story. He told us how one day when he had gone to hug his grown-up daughter she had flinched away from him, and burst out, 'You are the father to all our people, but you have never had the time to be a father to me'.

There it was—the one against the other: their work, our needs, their commitments, our lives, there was no squaring the circle. They knew it, somewhere, all their generation: as the state had poured out its wrath, they had watched their children suffer.

And yet, and yet—what else could they have done?

Gillian Slovo, on the death of her father, Joe Slovo, *Every Secret Thing: My Family, My Country* (1997)

This is one possible explanation, yet it requires support from another, based in an understanding of the forms of bodily repression and Victorian-type modesty that characterized the colonial/apartheid system. To be sure, Mandela did not entirely deny his desires: in sport and in his relationships with women he took a warm if covert pleasure in the erotic body and in emotional expression. A prominent sign of this pleasure, a *National Geographic* photograph of a bare-breasted, prancing Andaman Islander, whom he called Neolitha, stood for years on his desk in his Robben Island cell in order, he said, to make Winnie 'jealous' (Figure 16). When in the mornings he dusted Winnie's picture, standing alongside this one, and pressed his nose to hers in the

Nelson Mandela

16. Mandela's desk and bookcase in Cell No. 5, Robben Island Section B, photographed in 1978. Note the ripening tomatoes, the photograph of Winnie in traditional dress, the lively *National Geographic* picture of an Andaman Islander, for which fellow prisoner Mac Maharaj made the frame, the standard-issue South African desk calendar, in which he would note down appointments, and his folded prison blanket.

photo as he once had done in reality, he would feel again 'the electric current that used to flush through my blood' (Figure 13).

Frantz Fanon broke important theoretical ground in his 1952 *Black Skin, White Masks* when he observed that colonial governance operated through the control and management of bodies: the representation of the colonized as all-body—animalistic, savage—was central to colonialism's structure of values. Apartheid, a particularly acute form of colonial oppression, went so far as to declare the black body expendable, acting upon it with extreme violence. As the philosopher Achille Mbembe observes, extending Fanon's reading, colonial mastery required the absolute denial of the other human being: brutality defined the horizons of colonized existence. From this it followed, he contends, that resistance was most powerfully achieved, and liberation effected, when the colonized denied themselves, their own bodies, and brought themselves into confrontation with death—as did Mandela in the conclusion to his Rivonia Trial speech. Otherwise put, if the current conditions of life were inimical to freedom, winning freedom had to involve overcoming or cancelling life itself.

This perception illuminates Mandela's abiding interest in two moments in Shakespeare when death is described as inexorable. It may also illuminate the forcefulness with which ideals like freedom and justice are asserted in his prose. In *Julius Caesar* II.ii, Caesar invokes death as 'a necessary end' that 'will come when it will come'. This passage Mandela autographed as his favourite in Sonny Venkatrathnam's *Collected Shakespeare*, acknowledging that these were words that encompassed his acceptance of the authority of death. Yet his sense of a person's death as following a script as much as does their life is even more clearly evoked in the speech from *Measure for Measure* III.i, in which the Duke instructs Claudio, 'Be absolute for death'. These were lines that Mandela pondered while awaiting the Rivonia sentence, and, indeed, Claudio's words to the Duke directly preceding this command had already appeared as the resounding conclusion to his court speech: 'But if needs be, it is an ideal for which *I am prepared to die*'.

Counterpointing the authority granted to death, an equally important element in the historical process of black liberation struggle was the effort to recover the self—an effort that can also be read into Mandela's concern to safeguard his emotional being. His public discourse confronted the hostility to the black body of the apartheid system by choosing, strategically if defensively, to absent that body, to give way to an apparently excessive modesty. He resisted the apartheid obsession with the oppressed's so-called corporeality by neatly removing the African body from public consideration, asserting an ethical stance instead. His determination in doing so was no doubt facilitated by his never having been physically tortured while in prison, yet it is no less uncompromising for all that. His autobiographical language, too, is noticeably free of physical and emotional reference. His is strictly non-confessional prose, and as such it contrasts even with the writing of his model, the always professional, emotionally costive Nehru.

Mandela absorbed apartheid's impact on the body of the oppressed by, in effect, embracing its negations, as exemplified in the punishing regime to which he subjected himself from an early age, in prison as at school. The Mandela body may have been full of style, but it was also always disciplined. On Robben Island he rose every day at 3.30 a.m. for two hours of exercise. At Victor Verster and thereafter his schedule remained almost unchanged. In as much as the colonial state operated through forcing individual bodies to internalize its rules, Mandela effectively outdid it at that process of internalization. As the next chapter shows, he survived stringent circumstances by excelling at stringency.

Your beautiful photo still stands about two feet above my left-shoulder as I write this note. I dust it carefully every morning for doing so gives me the pleasant feeling that I'm caressing you as in the old days. I even touch your nose with mine to recapture the electric current that used to flush through my blood whenever I did so. Neolitha stands on the table directly opposite me. How can my spirits ever be down when I enjoy the fond attention of such wonderful ladies?

Nelson Mandela, from a letter to Winnie Mandela (May 1979)

Chapter 7

Spectres in the prison garden

Three images from the spectral island garden:

Working in the prison's blinding-white lime quarry Mandela
and his fellow prisoners were by the day's end covered in a
layer of snowy dust. To one another they appeared as ghosts.

Over a decade's digging in this same quarry damaged
Mandela's eyes, as it did his comrades'. In his case the
damage blocked his tear-ducts, which meant he could not
cry tears. His tears, even at times of sorrow, were invisible
tears—phantom tears.

Until the early 1980s visits from Mandela's family,
including Winnie, were strictly 'non-contact'. In a letter to
his daughter Zindzi, in which he mentioned her paying a
visit to Cape Town, he suggested she look across Table
Bay to Robben Island and imagine him there. Many of his
fellow South Africans would do the same through his
eighteen years of offshore incarceration, during which
almost no photographs of the island inmates were released
into the public domain. To his dear ones as to the nation at
large, Prisoner 466/64, the inmate of Cell No. 5, became in
effect a bodiless, intangible presence: a spectre, a ghost.

* * *

Against the earlier portrait of Mandela the flamboyant performer, this chapter considers his prison years 1962–90, chiefly the time in Robben Island Maximum Security Prison, but also in Pollsmoor and Victor Verster, a period abruptly separated from the vital 1950s, yet as significant to his formation. Mandela, it is important to remember, was incarcerated for a longer period than his political mentors Gandhi and Nehru—though they were imprisoned more frequently. And his time in prison was itself characterized by sharply contrastive features, which group into three clusters.

First, there were the predominant spectral qualities of life on the island, which include the at first almost dreamlike instances of cooperation between prisoners and warders, counterweighed by, second, the rigid, often brutal regime of everyday existence. Third, there were the important transformative aspects of the incarceration, which emerge from this combination of rough physicality and the ghostly-though-human. These aspects are bound up in the activity of gardening, of drawing life, colour, hope, and sustenance out of dirt, which was so important to Mandela throughout his twenty-seven and a half prison years. Gardening, as it turned out, offered him a practical correlative to his visions of change. He learned through cultivation to give concrete form to his dreams (so resembling many other dispossessed, as theorist Hélène Cixous writes).

At the time Mandela entered prison he was a hot-headed, opinionated young leader, given to pedantry, full of derivative ideas—as he himself confessed in a 20 June 1970 letter to his wife. He emerged from these secluded years reflective, disciplined, able to force a consensus and yet to draw the humanity out of another by his sheer conviction and persistence. What was the chemistry of the otherworldly and the down-to-earth that brought about this change? For it was by no means a foregone conclusion that Mandela would step out of prison as he eventually appeared: dignified, thoughtful, exceptionally free from bitterness, secure in the knowledge that, as he said, 'a simple exposition of principles' sheds light on 'universal truths'.

Ghosts and the regime

Besides clothes, bedding and our bailies [chamber pots], we had nothing else in our cells. We had to observe strict silence in our section. At weekends and on public holidays we were locked up for 24 hours at a stretch, with 30 minutes of exercise in the morning and another 30 minutes in the afternoon. During the week we would break stones in the yard, or work in the quarry, from 8:00 a.m. to 4:00 p.m.

We were locked up at 4:30 p.m. and would have our supper in our cells. By 8:00 p.m. we all had to be asleep. The lights remained on throughout the night and a warder locked in the section with us kept us under observation . . . from the corridor.

Eddie Daniels, from *There and Back* (1998)

Robben (Seal) Island, which lies about 6 miles from the city of Cape Town, washed by treacherous currents, had been used as a place of banishment from the time of early Dutch colonization. It carries its full complement of legends of haunting. There is the fearsome *Flying Dutchman* phantom schooner that plies these waters, and the story of the Malayan spiritual leader, the Prince of Madura, who died here (whose shrine stands nearby the prison). There is the drowned nun who is seen when the fog lies heavy around the Cape of Storms. The first to be exiled to the island was the Khoi interpreter (and only successful escapee) Autshumao in 1658. During the devastating 19th-century Xhosa land wars, the British authorities confined rebels here, including Mandela's ancestor Chief Makhanda. Already marked as a dumping ground for society's excluded, the island housed a leper colony and a lunatic asylum between 1844 and 1913. Twenty-nine ships have been wrecked off its shores.

Today, the 'World Heritage' Robben Island complex, the small town, leper graveyard, and the two main blocks of prison buildings (once separating common-law from political prisoners), has the drab aspect of other former places of incarceration and suffering: Dachau and Auschwitz, the West African slave forts. Yet, although unthreatening, even old-fashioned, in appearance, this place, no-one can forget, was once experienced as a claustrophobic hell. It was without comfort, without contact with the outside world, seemingly without hope, as the prison memoirs of Neville Alexander and Ahmed Kathrada, amongst others, describe, and Fugard, Kani, and Ntshona's striking play *The Island* (1974) still evokes.

During their time in this place of pariahs, shut out of history, Mandela and his comrades became to all intents and purposes living ghosts—to borrow a definition (used in another context) from Jacques Derrida's *Spectres of Marx*. Up until the 1980s' Free Mandela Campaign, they were from the viewpoint of their country 'not present, nor presently living'. Likewise, to them their country and its people had been turned into distant presences whom they would in all likelihood never see again, and certainly not touch, not as before: they were sentenced *for life*. They populated the past and invoked visions of the future, but the present was not theirs.

As the repressive 1960s wore on, the news blackout in South Africa was so entire that, historian Thomas Karis writes, the ANC organization, in disarray, became a mere 'shadowy presence'. The government 'wanted us to be forgotten by the outside world', island inmate Eddie Daniels remembers. In the refrain of Ghanaian Abena Busia's 1990 poem of homage, 'Testament for the First Accused', the ANC leader, 'still alive', 'still not free', subsists invisibly on the island while on the world stage major events in pan-African history take place—Martin Luther King's death; Mozambique's independence.

Thick walls separate the individual cells of Robben Island's Section B beside its concrete courtyard where leadership prisoners like Mandela were held. When prisoners were locked up at 4.30 p.m. each day, communication between the cells was virtually impossible. Until the mid-1970s, when the bedding was improved, they would lay themselves to sleep on two stiff blankets and a sisal mat. Many lived in dread of weekends, which were times of near-total isolation. Other political prisoners were held in large, crowded dormitories within the same block and, unlike the 'elite' prisoners, were exposed to arbitrary assaults by common-law inmates as well as warders. The food was universally poor: for Africans, mainly maize porridge and a watery yeast-drink. If the prisoners expressed grievances about the food, as with their favoured form of the hunger strike, they were assaulted. In 1965, the prisoners were moved from stone-breaking in the courtyard to work chipping lime. For the next fourteen years this activity took up every working day.

Many prisoners unsurprisingly felt beset by a sense of disorientation and disembodiedness, of being evacuated from society and history: that is, of being reduced to spectres. They not only spent long periods in silence, they also were deprived of watches, the most basic facility of self-regulation. Removed from the rest of the world's clock-time, they were obliged to give themselves up to the prison system's time regime, controlled by sirens and whistles, the half-hourly counting of the inmates, and the ever-burning light bulb. Until 1979 they were denied access to news or newspapers, another important medium through which a community understands itself in relation to the unfolding of history. Many filched papers from warders, memorized the news and transferred it verbally, or bartered tobacco for papers with common-law inmates, though they were severely punished if discovered.

D category prisoners, the Rivonia trialists' classificatory designation, were allowed one letter and one family visit every six months. Letters were arbitrarily censored and diaries, too, were confiscated. A third of the first draft of Mandela's autobiography—written at night from 1975 to 1976 at a rate of ten pages a day, copied by Maharaj and Chiba in minuscule handwriting—was discovered buried in document containers in the courtyard garden and confiscated. His 'life' was quite concretely taken from him—though the bulk of it appropriately remained hidden in the garden. (The smuggled copy, though it reached England, was not published.) As for visits, the thick glass-partition through which visitor faced prisoner made physical contact impossible. Family members spoke to one another strictly in English, via a telephone system with a warder listening on a third handset.

Even though the Island high command maintained contact with the exiled ANC by way of secret messages, crucial events on the mainland, like the Soweto uprising, were first communicated to the prisoners by means of curious omissions in their routine or unexplained punishments. In this respect, once again, they felt removed from history. For example, on 16 June 1976, the day of the uprising, their supply of hot water was inexplicably cut off. From this alone they were able to deduce that something momentous had taken place. Mandela wrote to Winnie: 'Sometimes I feel like one who is on the sidelines . . . who has missed life itself'.

An inextricable part of this phantom-like existence was that memory grew acute, as many reported. Images of the past cropped up as if alive. 'Here the past literally rushes to memory and there is plenty of time for reflection', Mandela commented. There was a prevalent feeling that people far away were in fact present, which made dreams vivid and often painful. From 1976 Mandela was beset by a recurring anxiety nightmare in which he returned to his old house at 8115 Ngakane Street, Orlando, to find the place deserted. 'Finally I would see my home, but it turned out to be empty, a ghost house, with all the doors and windows open but no one there at all'. The nightmare was uncannily prescient: the house was gutted by fire in 1988, the piece of wedding-cake Winnie had saved for Nelson's return lost. And once he did finally return to his longed-for house, it was to realize in a matter of weeks that his marriage was irretrievably over: his dream image had been an uncanny haunting.

In the early years, prisoners were not permitted to speak with one another while working in the quarry, but, with time, these regulations were relaxed. The change was largely a consequence of persistent prisoner complaints as the Section B inmates, all seasoned political campaigners, did not scruple to lodge grievances. In the silence of their cells they self-consciously learned how much was to be gained in terms of both moral and pedagogical support from structured dialogue, especially with fellow inmates. From the mid-1960s, study privileges being granted, the more formally educated prisoners began to disseminate economic theory and ANC history to their peers via *sotto voce* tutorials conducted while chipping lime. Although these privileges could be arbitrarily suspended, a kind of corporate prison life had by 1969 been established, with regular discussion groups and, on Sundays, board games and sports. To 'buy' reading time in his cell, Mandela contrived a system of bribing bored night-warders with copies of the women's housekeeping magazine *Huisgenoot* (to which his Afrikaans studies entitled him).

A mission-school product, Mandela appears to have found he could most successfully survive Robben Island's rigours by internalizing them. Amongst his fellow inmates he was well-known for having effected this internalization with near-total success, bar the few times he registered personal bereavement or insult. Into this internalization—what Wole Soyinka calls his 'logic'—it is possible to read the classic response of the child separated early from their home environment: the cultivation of an inner steeliness became a crucial survival mechanism, which, in prison, Mandela deployed mercilessly. His inmate colleagues, including close friends like Kathrada, remarked on his growing aloofness and impenetrability across the island years: how he channelled his anger into intellectual argument; how he watched the prison authorities like a hawk. If as a student he had embraced the Victorian work ethic, and if as a lawyer-in-training he had virtually recreated himself through self-discipline (as in his gym routines), he now sought to embody steeliness.

Only occasionally, especially when brooding on family relationships in letters home, did he confess to an insufficiency of the 'steel' he required. To family friend Frieda Matthews he spoke of the 'thousand wounds' a man might carry in his heart. Eddie Daniels observed how he sometimes wrapped himself tight in a blanket, as if to cauterize an inner pain. With trusted friends like Daniels he liked to quote as a correlative for his survival-by-rigour his staple 'Invictus'. Among the other products of imperialist-amputee Henley's pen is the jingoistic collection *For England's Sake*, published to whip up British fervour for the Boer War. Yet in 'Invictus', taken on its own, Mandela clearly found his ethic of self-mastery given compelling expression within the frame of a controlled rhyme-scheme supported by strong, monosyllabic nouns. It was only a small step from espousing this poem to assuming a Victorian persona, as he could do in letters to his children. In ways they predictably found alienating, he tried to press them to ever-greater effort, reiterating that ambition and drive were the only means of escaping an 'inferior position' in life.

However, as many of the prisoners found, it was within this formidably abstracted yet also disciplined environment, far more than in the political hurly-burly of Soweto, that ideas might be held up for sustained inspection and thoroughly analysed, explored through discussion and in the round. It was in relation to their ghostly dimension of mere living-on—Derrida's dimension of the dead and future generations, but also of prisoners-for-life— that concepts of justice and dignity were most clearly to be comprehended, unrestricted by the circumstances of finite, ordinary life. As Mandela himself wrote in the essay, 'National Liberation': '[Here] [o]ne is able to stand back and look at the entire movement from a distance.'

Put differently, Robben Island confined Mandela to the realm of the symbolic, which earlier he had already learned skilfully to manipulate for the purposes of legal advocacy. Now he found it a medium in which his political intellect could move with special facility, as when he attempted to approach others' perspectives, including his warders', on their own merits, or identified at different levels with both Creon and Antigone in the Island production of Sophocles' eponymous play. Among prisoner friends he was well-known for his tendency to meditate on a move in chess for days at a time: his style 'deliberate', his strategy 'conservative', as he himself admitted. He was noted, too, for the patience with which he pursued discussion, relying on his capacity for listening and avoiding judgement, corroborating the other speaker's position with occasional remarks, pushing them gradually to concede common ground.

Once, when inducting the SWAPO leader Toivo ja Toivo into how argument worked on the Island, Mandela provocatively advised him to 'engage all and sundry in conversation, during which he could make political points'. Particularly difficult debates, as between the ANC and PAC or, later, with Black Consciousness adherents, Mandela liked to imagine three-dimensionally, as a drama played out in a theatre. This capacity to focus at length, if anything, deepened over the years, as he learned a new sensitivity to others' needs. His approach was counter-intuitive, Jakes Gerwel observed, thinking of a challenge from several sides so as to come to a more robust conclusion. Indeed, his critics later suggested, henceforth Mandela was to conclude that most problems, including difficult economic questions post-apartheid, could be solved through the careful balancing of different options, as if the problem were an impasse in an Island board game.

Signs of the abstraction of the Island prisoners' thought are found in the pristine state of Mandela's law books. Although most of the heavy tomes bear signs of having been read, and are neatly wrapped in protective plastic, Mandela's marginal 'notes' are restricted to the occasional small tick, marking a place in his reading. Though prisoners tended to avoid note-making in order not to be censured, it is here as if case law or jurisprudence were being looked at purely in-and-for-itself, in principle, a code removed from the considerations of state.

Author's observation on Mandela's law books, Mayibuye-Robben Island Archive (2006)

As a group, too, the Section B prisoners indulged their pleasure in exploring ideas—of law, democracy, freedom—at almost indefinite length. They found that their regime of enforced silence and proximity pushed them to establishing rules of decorum for confronting their political differences, while their disciplined dialogic mode imparted a new sense of intellectual authority. Rank-and-file political prisoners assisted the discussion in a special way, by copying out verbatim extracts from history and political science, for dissemination through the wider group (a practice that continued until the last political prisoners left the island). From their position as spectres removed from time—family, sex, getting, spending—yet with time on their hands, the prisoners were able to gain perspective, too, on countervailing points of view. Within the unvarying rhythm of the island's days, positions could be endlessly restated, and eventually subtly revised in relation to one another. Recapitulation, because inevitable, was acceptable and clarifying, especially where viewpoints were diametrically opposed.

In a nutshell, their prison situation allowed these intellectually disciplined, politically experienced men to ponder political problems and processes (resistance, negotiation) in detail and from every available angle, literally for years. As Fran Buntman suggests in her Robben Island study, the prisoners' efforts to set up an orderly political microcosm transformed their incarceration from a reactive, prohibitive experience into a productive social contract. Their methods—the codes of exchange they established—would prove fundamental to how Mandela arrived at his 'negotiating concept' in the mid-1980s.

Essentially, Section B constituted in itself nothing so much as a ready-made seminar group or think-tank, a development the apartheid state had not foreseen, certainly not before Mandela's move to Pollsmoor. As well as his Rivonia group of mostly well-educated friends, Mandela was here surrounded by members of the other liberation parties, especially the PAC but also Maoists and Trotskyists, similarly concerned to study the political process, talk about change, and map areas of agreement. As Minister of Justice Kobie Coetsee brusquely conceded: 'the real effect [of putting them together on Robben Island] was to build them'.

There is nothing like a long spell in prison to focus your mind, and to bring you to a more sober appreciation of the realities of your society.

Mandela to the Commonwealth Eminent Persons Group, 1986

Yet to describe Robben Island's 'University' with an accent on structured dialogue is not to suggest that a Socratic concord prevailed at all times. In the 1960s and 1970s, Mandela disagreed vehemently with radical Marxists like Mbeki and Gwala about such questions as the place of nationalism within a socialist struggle, and the merits of violent 'seizure' as against negotiation. Especially after 1976, with the arrival of Black Consciousness prisoners, discussion was often extremely heated. Mandela concentrated on talking through ANC differences with the exclusivist BCM with an unwavering commitment, commanding the new prisoners' respect with his rationalism and understanding for their youthful energy. In him they saw, as Seth Mazibuko remembered, how the 'bright and shiny instrument' of self-discipline might shape a way into the future.

The painstaking deliberations of prison appear to have sharpened the inmates' conviction of their eventual success. A 1981 Justice Department report on Mandela noticed that imprisonment had failed to dent his idealism or undermine his self-belief. He never doubted that the span of his active life would coincide with the timescale of fundamental change. The prison cell's processes of deliberate, empathetic introspection also brought the important insight that apartheid did not represent simply a case of raw colonial repression, but entailed also the defensive nationalist struggle of the Afrikaner *volk* to retain hold of their hard-won power. For the ANC, therefore, it was necessary to tackle this defensiveness head-on. Discussion especially with warders seems to have reinforced Mandela's faith in the advantages of a multi-pronged resistance movement. In 1981 or 1985, as in 1964, or even 1952, the armed struggle in his view was to be engaged *alongside* mass mobilization. Once newspapers and political histories were made available to him, he was able to learn from the fate of independence movements elsewhere in Africa how difficult it was for an anti-colonial movement to institutionalize itself as a political party after independence. Hence the need to make accommodations with the party in power.

Yet dialogic games of position and manoeuvre were not Mandela's sole distraction from prison routine. As well as the hidden joys of his letters home, there were, later, at Pollsmoor and Victor Verster, the small indulgences provided by friends and warders, like fishcakes and poached egg for breakfast, and Romany Cream biscuits. He particularly enjoyed the biriyanis Kathrada prepared, which recalled the food Indian Congress activists had supplied during his time underground. The presence of nature on the island, too, offered poignant sources of inspiration: the sea views and birds, the strong, sweeping winds. A rare sighting of the night sky, when the prisoners were once allowed into the prison yard after dark, many remembered as revelatory. Finally, there was to Mandela in particular the relief provided by his gardening hobby, in which his propensity for careful deliberation found external expression in the slow processes of working with seeds and soil.

Transformation in a garden

Your patience grows inhuman, Mandela.
Do you grow food? Do you make friends
Of mice and lizards? Measure the growth of grass
For time's unhurried pace?
Are you now the crossword puzzle expert?

Wole Soyinka, from 'Your Logic Frightens Me, Mandela', *Mandela's Earth* (1988)

In his often-quoted 'Your Logic Frightens Me, Mandela', the poet Soyinka imagines the world's famous political prisoner cultivating patience and honing his idealism by means of the quiet watchfulness demanded of gardeners. Soyinka's speculations were prescient: within Robben Island's barrenness, Mandela had begun a garden.

Given how many prison hours were spent in introspective seclusion, gardening became especially important to Mandela, as it has to other political prisoners, as a link with the material world. The activity of working a garden, of keeping in contact with the earth, in many ways corroborated the processes of regeneration to which he looked forward. As well as relaxation and enjoyment, gardening afforded a correlative for the strategies of political transformation he was sketching in his mind. There was an alchemy of freedom-through-reconstruction (rather than revolution) to be had in growing things. It also, crucially, marked the passing of the seasons.

Mandela had acquired some experience of gardening from both his time at Clarkebury Institute and tending the garden at Liliesleaf Farm, Rivonia, where his alias David Motsamayi masked as a gardener. At Clarkebury, he wrote in his autobiography, helping in Reverend Harris's garden not only 'planted in me a lifelong love of... growing vegetables', but also, importantly, it permitted closer human contact than was possible beyond its cooperative parameters: 'it helped me get to know the reverend and his family'.

Building on these early experiences, Mandela on Robben Island approached the cultivation of a garden in the same way as in 1961/2 he had set out to become a guerrilla fighter: that is, systematically and by the book, 'by reading and talking to the experts'. Towards the mid-1970s, he and his MK commander Laloo Chiba, known to have green fingers, were granted permission to use as their garden space a strip of opened ground at the far end of the concrete prison yard, at right angles to the Section B corridor (Figure 17). As well as reading any advice manuals he could lay his hands on, Mandela began to measure beds, and weigh and grind compost. The garden was to be productive, not merely decorative: it would grow nutritious vegetables for the prisoners. The prison warders were persuaded to supply seeds (though they were later susceptible to raiding the garden when the prisoners were locked up).

17. The southern end of the Robben Island 'Section B' prison yard, the location of the vegetable garden that Mandela worked along with Laloo Chiba.

Before long, the prison garden was run as a full-scale operation. By late 1975, Mandela, Chiba, and their helpers had raised 2,000 chillies, 1,000 tomatoes, and two watermelons, as well as peppers and cucumbers. In a photograph of Mandela's cell taken around this time, ripening tomatoes and peppers are clearly on view, laid out on his desk (Figure 16). Included as the keynote image in the collection of archive photographs, *A Prisoner in the Garden* (2004), the 1977 photograph of Mandela as prison gardener was taken against his will, in a location that was not his garden, yet it, too, stands as an evocative image of this time (Figure 18). Here we see the political prisoner laying claim to a patch of ground, his island rock, a piece of his nation, by making it fruitful. In the eyes of the world he may be an invisible man, yet in his small garden he is engaged, immediate to himself, fully occupying the present moment.

Despite the at-first-unpromising conditions, the shift to the cells on the concrete roof of Pollsmoor Prison interrupted but did not

18. **The prisoner in the island garden: a 1977 photograph of Mandela (alongside others) involved in gardening work.**

curtail Mandela's gardening activities. Prisoner D220/82 (as 466/64 had now become) undertook to relieve the rooftop's grey monotony by creating a 'garden in the sky' using sixteen 44-gallon oil drums sawn in half, into which he poured soil carted from the prison's own market garden. Once again, he obsessively watched over the development of the eventual 900 plants, helped by his Rivonia colleagues. Once again, warders, including the prison commander, supplied seeds and assisted with erecting hessian barriers against the Cape wind. Echoing the autobiography, prison warder James Gregory observed:

> Eventually, at the height of the growing season, there was a huge variety of plants in the vegetable section: aubergines, cabbage, beans, spinach, carrots, cucumbers, onions, broccoli, lettuce, tomatoes of a number of varieties…and many types of spices.

Mandela gave satchels-full of fresh vegetables to the warders, and supplied the kitchen with produce for a 'special' Sunday meal. His gardening granted him, he recounted, an almost god-like sense of reshaping the world. 'The bible tells us that gardens preceded gardeners, but that was not the case at Pollsmoor': here he created a 'far grander' garden than that at Robben Island.

At his last place of incarceration, as was fitting, a garden was laid on for Mandela's sole use. His deputy governor's cottage at Victor Verster came with an established 'idyllic' garden to care for, though its wall was raised to screen his activities from passers-by. Even on the day of his release, he took time to show his family and friends the vegetables and now also flowers he had cultivated.

How do we explain the sustained importance of gardening to the prisoner Mandela? For one, from the perspective of a self-styled 'country boy', the pleasures of working the earth no doubt recalled the rural environment of his childhood, evoked in nostalgic terms in his letters. For another, in his garden he could practise prudence, self-sufficiency, and provident planning. The etymology of the word *husbandry* signifies both farming and 'resourceful management' (*OED*)—specifically, in Mandela's terms, building cooperation and an independent life out of unproductive conditions. Within the spectral seclusion imposed by the life sentence, gardening also allowed the prisoner to explore the *spirit* of certain key ideas—of regeneration and reconstruction, for example—in a reassuringly *gritty*, material medium.

It is telling, though probably coincidental, that two major southern African novels of the period, Bessie Head's *A Question of Power* (1974), and J. M. Coetzee's *Life and Times of Michael K* (1983), find in the activity of gardening a potent symbol of endurance and new life. In a country divided by conflict, the distraction of gardening could of course represent a questionable refusal of politics, yet it equally signified a position from which to proceed beyond conflict, to reshape the world, even if in a small way.

In *A Question of Power*, the 'full-time work' of a communal garden project represents psychological healing after a punishing period of madness. In cataloguing, seeding, planting, watering—in gooseberries, tomatoes, cauliflower—Elizabeth, the protagonist, discovers a confirmation of the ordinary that opens her heart to a feeling of unity with humankind. Coetzee's K, a vagrant 'Gardener, Grade 1', on the run from a series of institutions and camps, explores through the 'exultant' cultivation of his pumpkins, squashes, and melons a means of transitory survival, an important source of continuity between the past and the present, the earth and animal life. For him it is also, significantly, a way of evading the camps that threaten to fence him round.

With his cultivation of a patch of earth—discovering a common love of soil and plant-rearing with his captors—Mandela developed important insights into the qualities of forbearance and cooperation, and into the accommodations that eventual mastery, including self-mastery, would entail. He commented:

> In prison, a garden is one of the few things you can really master and call your own...The feeling of being the steward of this tiny patch of earth is a small taste of freedom.

As well as supplying a life-affirming sanctuary away from, if enclosed by, the morbid prison world, husbanding a garden could, in other words, assume certain of the aspects of creating a self-sufficient community or fostering a nation—as well as remaking a self. Coaxing life out of the earth, Mandela saw that mere ruthlessness would prove inimical to national unity: law would always be more constructive than war. In a 1976 letter, he suggestively used an image of a growing plant as a symbol for political work.

At an interpersonal level, too, gardening provided a space where common interests between prisoner and warder could be plotted, and Mandela's early conviction that 'all men have a core of decency' explored. It is probably true to say that gardening, this one opportunity for 'free', constructive activity, became the primary dimension through which Mandela perceived that the mutual recognition of *humanness*—the regenerative concept of *ubuntu*—was fundamental to national transformation. Taking these different perspectives together, we see how it was in prison that he moved decisively away from thinking in terms of received ideas of the political struggle as a racially polarized conflict.

If we accept that Mandela's gardening contributed to how he set about forging a new political understanding for South Africa, we discern in the process an example of how he transformed his practice into a theory of national reconciliation, something that must count among his primary achievements. Just as he worked to convert the island's 'culture of dialogue' (Soyinka's phrase) into a strategy of negotiation, the work of practical husbandry, too, translated into the painstaking vigilance with which he approached his government interlocutors, introducing his views to them, keeping them talking, yet consulting with the ANC.

The historian Antoinette Burton's work on the relation of the domestic space to the unfolding of public history suggests that the enclosed structure of an individual's living environment determines their understanding of both family and national life. Her theory can be applied to how a long-term political prisoner like Mandela interacted with national history from his spartan cell: to how he derived protocols for action from working the confined yet adaptive and creative spaces of his garden plots.

Mac Maharaj once summarized his leader's style of debate as 'proceeding from *their* assumptions and carefully marshalling arguments to move them to his conclusions. His line of advance [was] developed on the other party's line of attack': it was an intensely strategic, and spatialized, approach. As this suggests, shut away together with a group of trusted interlocutors committed to one-to-one dialogue, Mandela's situation moulded his eventual rules of engagement with the Afrikaner government. It shaped the parameters—accommodating, other-directed, determined and secretive, but open-ended—within which he set about mapping the road to a national peace.

As with his prison cell, so, too, with his gardens. His cultivation projects read Mandela a lesson in proceeding with patience and caution, yet productively also. The man who once, as a political leader on the run, had no home life to speak of and certainly no time for a garden, now learned to appreciate the values of slowness, tactility, and proximity, of incremental change and the simple bonds of human cooperation. In this there is a partial analogy with how Gandhi used the feminine task of spinning *khadi* yarn to articulate his politics. In Mandela's case, however, his gardening did not represent a public performance or political declaration. The position of pragmatic reformism he arrived at via his gardening and prison dialogues was learned intuitively, day-to-day, and on the job, without ostentation. Moreover, as his long-term 'home' was not in fact homely or welcoming, he developed a particularly intimate, even proprietorial, relationship

to his wider national home, South Africa, to the extent of acting
unilaterally once the time came to rescue that home from
civil war.

> Go end there
> One fine day
> Where never till then
> Till as much as to say
> No matter where
> No matter when
>
> Samuel Beckett, 'Brief Dream', in *For Nelson Mandela* (1986)

Chapter 8
Mandela's legacy

In Lewis Nkosi's 2006 *Bildungsroman, Mandela's Ego*, the Zulu boy Dumisa grows up with the sense of Mandela as his life-mentor and second father—the invisible household spirit shaping his life. Until recently, many South Africans could have been described in the same terms as Dumisa. Mandela was the story many lived and, in some cases, died by. His legacy seemed unassailable. However, events in the later 2010s impacted his posthumous reputation—though not fatally, I would argue. Though South Africans have for some time confronted a future without Mandela, he remains a governing national myth, a model of personal sacrifice and reconciliation.

Within hours of Mandela's death in December 2013 becoming public, both impromptu and curated shrines cropped up on South African street corners, including outside his Johannesburg home (Figure 19). His lying-in-state in Pretoria was attended by thousands who waited long hours and filed past in silence to pay their respects. Many prominent world leaders, of all political stripes, attended his funeral, including Dilma Rousseff and Barack Obama, also the first black leader of his country, for whom Mandela was a beacon of 'progress'. Mandela had lapsed gradually from the world, but when he was laid to rest in his natal earth, his sign quickly became something greater than human. His long-anticipated apotheosis seemed to be complete.

> His sacrifice was so great that it called upon people everywhere
> to do what they could on behalf of human progress...In the
> most modest of ways, I was one of those people who tried to
> answer his call.

Barack Obama, *New Yorker* (27 June 2013)

19. Mandela's shrine.

It is hard now to credit how widespread and whole-hearted that
reverence was. There are few national heroes whose reputations
remain untarnished for very long after their death, but in
Mandela's case the judgement of history moved quickly, and even
his ethical contribution proved vulnerable to critique. How will
the future assess Madiba, considering this new public
ambivalence? How assured will his reputation as a battler for
freedom and justice remain? This chapter explores his
posthumous trajectory, and urges that, in the end, he continues to
stand as an inspiring symbol of humanism, perseverance, and
hope, perhaps even as a beacon of creative inspiration.

* * *

The earth's trembling, gentlemen!
the rivers all roaring
the mountains all shaking
mighty nations are puzzled,
for small nations are writhing,
straining, striving to burst their bonds.
The earth's surely trembling,
the earth's surely trembling.
Hacker in thorn brakes,
scything swathes through ignorance;
colossus astride the earth;
rocker rocking the land,
chanti encoiling it,
snake that swims the Vaal,
but sips the Zambezi;
servant of Africa's nations.

From *imbongi* / praise-singer David Manisi, 'Chief Rohihlahla Nelson Mandela (Hail, Earth Tremor!)', 1954

In 1994, Nelson Mandela and his Government of National Unity founded the new South African republic on the basis of racial reconciliation and a new humanism. 'The sun shall never set on so glorious a human achievement', Mandela optimistically ended his 10 May inaugural address. His ethical republic was built on a fragile foundation. Most South African citizens were entirely unused to working within democratic structures, and the economy remained unreconstructed, with a narrow echelon of whites together with a new black middle-class minority in control of the country's capital. Moreover, especially with the massive corruption that tainted Jacob Zuma's presidency, Mandela's ANC, too, has suffered a reputational battering. The death and funeral of Emeritus Archbishop Desmond Tutu in December 2021, however, saw a significant reassessment of the legacy of reconciliation, with new attention paid to how, in 1994, this represented the least painful way forward for the country.

Mandela stood down as first democratic president in 1999. In the 21st century, his legacy is no longer as secure as it once was, despite official exhibitions that proclaim his virtues. This is due in great part to the South African state's mixed record on addressing the inequalities of the past, but it is also a consequence of how Mandela's approach now appears in the light of those disparities. Mandela's relatability and personal history succeeded in convincing a wide range of South Africans to support his 1990s negotiated settlement. A social chameleon, he strove to be all things to all people: an African nationalist among African nationalists, a socialist in relation to his SACP colleagues, and so on. But he was also the electioneering president-in-waiting who in 1994 catastrophically denied the emerging HIV/AIDS epidemic in South Africa so as not to lose votes for the already massively popular ANC.

In a desperately unequal society, Mandela's yen for performance and adaptability now appears from some angles as untrustworthy and too-changeable, pandering to those who continued to hold economic power, including internationally. Critics also see this changeability as negatively characterizing his presidential years. For example, while he advised his administration to seek an ethical foreign policy, he condoned the sale of South African-made armaments to countries like Algeria and Colombia whose human rights records were poor (but whose leaders had been ANC sympathizers).

> If there is any significant role that I played, it was that of being a vessel through which the struggle was presented to the nation and the world. The struggle had to have a symbol for it to be effective. The great men and women of the struggle chose that I be that symbol. If this was a good thing, praise must go to those who made the choice.
>
> Nelson Mandela, Interview with Oprah Winfrey (April 2001)

Despite his apparent malleability, at certain points, when Mandela deemed it historically expedient, he was not afraid to impose his vision, whether on supporters or opponents. This combination of broad receptivity with the occasional authoritarian impulse was determined in some measure by his overriding concern to achieve social harmony. He sought not to ignore differences so much as to set up moral codes that could be more or less agreed by all. On matters of common interest (armed struggle, negotiation, reconciliation), he could speak directly to his people. But his consensus-building also sometimes meant that he controversially took pains to view a conflict from the point of view of *the other*, as well as of his own party.

It remains clear that we must seek the lasting legacy of Mandela's long struggle for freedom in the domain of the political or ethical and not the economic. He stood for a great cause, the fight against apartheid. He responded to his country's need for redemption by presenting as a saviour figure (Figure 20). More practically, he proved to be, across his life, a far-sighted strategist and a powerful activist-thinker distinguished by fine moral intuitions. He never ceased to wrestle with, revise, and reclarify his political claims, all the while remaining aware of South Africa's need for the liberatory myth that he himself embodied. If Ghassan Hage is right in suggesting that a nation offers its citizens a sense of entitlement by offering them hope for the future, then among Mandela's key achievements is to have outlined new possibilities of hope for all South African citizens (though, his detractors say, some more than others).

Hope however meant compromise—and it is in the nature of that compromise that his reputation is most vulnerable. He did not deal equitably with black South Africans as against white in forging compromise. He did not insist upon the socialist state that the 1955 Freedom Charter proclaimed and he still claimed to espouse in the early 1990s. He chose not to found his country's new political equalities on the basis of social and

20. *Last Supper* by Rebecca Goldberg, 2007. Leaders of 20th-century South Africa of various political persuasions gather around Mandela the saviour figure in this witty pastiche of Leonardo da Vinci's painting.

economic policies that would erase or even mitigate entrenched patterns of uneven development. He wasted his hard-won moral capital. As Neville Alexander observes, the negotiated settlement Mandela presided over precluded the realization of some of the most modest electoral promises of reconstruction. For theorist Slavoj Žižek in December 2013, Mandela's 'universal glory is … a sign that he really didn't disturb the global order of power'. For 2010s #RhodesMustFall activists, he presided over, essentially, the full-scale privatization of apartheid.

The question then is: could Mandela or his government ever properly have honoured Freedom Charter promises? The abolition of apartheid represented a hugely ambitious project, involving thoroughgoing regime change and mind-shift at every level. In the context of the Cold War's end, some might contend, the success of South Africa's democratic experiment required a Faustian pact of adjustment to the neo-liberal world system. Which is to say, as Ghassan Hage, too, admits, new hope works well with capitalism.

> I have walked that long road to freedom. I have tried not to falter; I have made missteps along the way. But I have discovered the secret that after climbing a great hill, one only finds that there are many more hills to climb. I have taken a moment here to rest, to steal a view of the glorious vista that surrounds me, to look back on the distance I have come. But I can rest only for a moment, for with freedom come responsibilities, and I dare not linger, for my long walk is not yet ended.
>
> Nelson Mandela, final paragraph, *Long Walk to Freedom* (1995)

Humanist vision

At crucial points across his career, Mandela set himself up as the model of the selfsame political-ethical positions that he was working to achieve: justice, non-racialism, social understanding. He used his experiences to illustrate his politics, and was not averse to moulding his political image to fit in with his media representations, when this was helpful to his cause. His party corroborated this process by establishing, as the centrepiece of its ideological self-legitimation, the often-compensatory myth of Madiba as redemptive national leader. He became an imaginative force-field within which a variety of different constituencies could invest meaning. In post-millennium South African novels, such as Ndebele's *The Cry of Winnie Mandela*, or Dangor's *Bitter Fruit* (both 2003), as well as *Mandela's Ego* (2006), Mandela stalks through, now as intimidating legend, now as benign figure of authority. A decade on from these works, the poet-activist Koleka Putuma, too, even while attacking Mandela for his wasteful pandering to white people, nonetheless uses his name in her poetry as a watchword and an emblem:

> I want someone who is going to look at me
> and love me
> the way that white people look at
> and love
> Mandela.
> <#>
> Someone who is going to hold onto my memory
> the way white people hold onto Mandela's legacy.
> <#>
> A lover who will build Robben Island in my backyard
> and convince me that I have a garden
> and fresh air, a rainbow and freedom.
>
> Koleka Putuma, '1994: A Love Poem', *Collective Amnesia* (2017)

As we have seen throughout, Mandela-the-life courts a symbolic reading. It asks to be taken as an object lesson in social transformation—an always open-ended assertion of a new humanism. Mandela, over the years, found a way of converting his respect for the human dignity in each and every person into a political practice through dialogue, finding common ground and establishing mutual regard. For him, national reconciliation involved convincing South African citizens by example to act on the same respect.

As we look to the future, what do the lessons of Mandela's transformative postcolonial humanism entail both for the world and for his country? In what ways does he remain a model for 21st-century culture and politics?

> [Even that] old man with the smile of a mischievous child,
> Madiba, whom he once thought of as the saving grace of the
> older world: they all have the same brittle air of vulnerability, of
> souls fallow despite years of feverish cultivation. 'The struggle'
> sowed the seeds of bright hopes and burning ideals, but look at
> what they are harvesting: an ordinariness, but also a vanity fed
> by sly and self-seductive glimpses in the mirrors of their personal
> histories.
>
> Achmat Dangor, from *Bitter Fruit* (2003)

Continuing a development that began with his 1950s turn to
multiracialism, Mandela in gaol began to shift his understanding
of human identity from the partial and the racialized, to
something more universal and reciprocal. Moving through diverse
situations of one-to-one interaction, Mandela increasingly
approached others not as members of a certain party or group,
but as human beings first and foremost, as unpredictable,
complicated, yet always ethical (or potentially ethical) agents. He
became more interested in likeness than in difference; he focused
on interaction, not separation.

Whereas postcolonial thought in Africa has conventionally
focused on the polarized conflict of oppressor and oppressed,
Mandela restored the idea of the fellow human being—the
human perceived not as fixity, but as fluid, multifarious, poetic,
and, most importantly, defined through reciprocity. His political
vision essentially grew out of anti-colonial practice, yet it
developed through his prison dialogues and the negotiations with
his enemy into an ideal for involvement that defied antinomy.
This expanded understanding of his fellow human being
coordinates to an extent with the Christianized humanist concept
of *ubuntu* popularized by Desmond Tutu. This is reflected in
Tutu's Nguni saying *umntu ngumntu ngabantu*, that is, 'a person
is a person through other people', or 'my selfhood is contingent

upon your selfhood': *I am well **if** you are well.* In Mandela's case, the thought translates into his 1985 speech refusing Botha's conditional release, crystallized in the line: 'Your freedom and mine cannot be separated'. Such an adventurous openness to the other's humanness was self-evidently anathema to the apartheid system.

Towards the end of *The Wretched of the Earth*, Fanon looks forward to the day when the new postcolonial nation will produce 'new men'. His conclusion speaks urgently of how the so-called Third World is to rehumanize the masses of humankind and rewrite history, not by imitating Europe, which always proceeds by way of deadly oppositions, but by making new, intensified, live connections.

Mandela contributed forcefully to the redefinition of the human proclaimed by Fanon, yet at the same time pulled it in a different direction. To the new humanism he added, first, the idea that black people remake themselves through forms and energies *other than*—or at least in addition to—those involved in death. That is to say, he disposed of Fanon's 'irrepressible violence' as a means of making history, and instead championed conversation, trust, and listening.

His second key contribution to the tantalizing definition of a reshaped humanism was subtly but determinedly to Africanize it, as in *ubuntu*, in the knowledge that humanism had always been defined against blackness. Reminding supporters and enemies alike of his Africanness, he translated humanism in line with the values of reciprocity and mutual support that had always lain at the heart of African socialism. As the pan-nationalist Aimé Césaire might have said, his was a humanism made to the measure *both* of the world *and* of Africa, defined from the perspective of those whose humanity had historically been denied. Radically, the African was at the centre of Mandela's concept of the human, *not* the margin or outside against which the human was understood.

Throughout, Mandela's refusal of doctrine gave him the opportunity to make challenging juxtapositions, such as of Africanness and rationality. As in his careful building of consensus, he interleaved aspects of African tradition with colonial modernity by casting these as already modern, yet unique and home-grown. African identity, he said in 1997, had always been 'the product of our engagement in world history'. He decisively placed Africa within a range of categories—sensibility, morality, justice—from which it had been excluded. His political methodology—witty, learned, deft—saw his continent in all its complexity as central to the narrative of world history.

Against this important legacy of African humanism, what of the charge that the compromise on which it was forged gave too much away, benefiting white people over black? Whereas on a world stage, as any global history shows, the name Mandela bears heroic status, by contrast, for many young South Africans today, especially those associated with the Fallist protests of the 2010s, its overriding keynotes are disillusionment and frustration. Even the beloved Madiba story can now appear suspect and dated, especially state-sanctioned as it is—by a state painfully exposed as dysfunctional and corrupt in the years since Mandela's death. By 2020, writes the critic Hedley Twidle, the Mandela years looked to younger generations as 'so last century' while the 1990s' deracialization project was written off as a folly and a dream. By contrast, Winnie Mandela's much less ambiguous message meant that her popularity among ANC and other voters remained untarnished despite the many scandals she faced (as her obituaries in April 2018 showed).

The meanings of any icon are attached to its history. One of the problems Mandela's reputation now faces is that it belongs to a period, the late twentieth century, when moral binaries of right and wrong were more clear-cut than they are today. Ours is not a time of redemptive and salutary life-stories, at least in politics.

His mediatized story may also appear to some as contaminated by the exact same processes of global marketing that once made it so ubiquitous. Posthumous official publications about Mandela like *Dare Not Linger* (2017), the so-called sequel to *Long Walk to Freedom*, or *I Remember Nelson Mandela* (2018), may only exacerbate this sense of discomfort. The books' neutral, balanced tone does little to address the questions that have arisen concerning Mandela's reputation.

Then again, Mandela was always intensely aware of the mortality of his own persona, and of the pace of history, as Sarah Nuttall and Achille Mbembe write. He always supported the need to 'move on' in political terms—the importance of one generation giving way to another. Just as he engaged with 1970s Black Consciousness activists on Robben Island, he would certainly have been interested in debating with the Fallist generation. When, in 2018 (his centenary year), the Nigerian-South African novelist Yewande Omotoso said 'Mandela opened something, now we can carry on', she expressed a sentiment he would have backed. He was consistently open to exploring risky, up-to-that-point unthinkable spaces whether in South African or international politics.

In 2021, a new sculpture 'Rona batho / We, the people' by the South African artist Mohau Modikaseng, was unveiled in Zuidoost, the Netherlands. In a neighbourhood that claims to be one of Europe's most diverse, this sculpture to Mandela's memory deliberately avoided representing Mandela himself. According to Modikaseng, Mandela was too familiar a subject, one in whom 'questions appear to have been answered'. Instead, the sculpture brings together seven faces, or facial fragments, from the surrounding community, set within an imperfect circle, precisely to deconstruct that sense of completeness Mandela epitomizes. The arrangement of the faces suggests a creative openness to the future, viewed from many different directions. The sculpture provides a provocative emblem on which to close, not least as it simultaneously still honours Mandela's struggle-era lessons in human reciprocity and consensus-building.

As the sculpture emphasizes, a key aspect of Mandela's vision was the capacity to take account of others, to see politics in the round. This capacity relates closely to the former president's facility for imaginative bricolage. While Nuttall and Mbembe speak of his life as a process of ceaseless transfiguration, it might also be helpful to think of his metamorphoses in more concrete terms, as a talent for inspired improvisation and eidetic political thought. Mandela had a capacity for combining two or more perspectives not normally associated together, creating a kind of charged relationality between them. He had a famously keen intuition for what can be termed dialogic field, for thinking 'sharply' beyond polarized viewpoints. He worked comfortably in the subjunctive tense, a notoriously difficult mode in which to operate, though it is this feature that now attracts criticism, the more so as he is not present (deftly, counter-intuitively) to defend himself.

To Edouard Glissant the Martinique theorist of creolization, a 'trembling' is perceived whenever the old order shifts, giving way to new, often risky, perceptions. Throughout his career, Mandela tuned into that trembling and made it conceivable for others. Far from standing in its way, he always sought to encourage such energy, even when it meant questioning his own most cherished ideas. He was at the end of the day a mould-breaker and a genre-bender. He was able empathetically yet pragmatically to enter into seemingly intractable problems and find ways of resolving them. He turned old templates into fluid new forms that younger generations might take forwards, always motivated by their own particular interests and passions, but inspired by his spirit and his grace.

It's impossible to make small talk with an icon
Which is why, to find my tongue,
I stare down at those crunched-up
One-time boxer's knuckles.
In their flattened pudginess I find
Something partly reassuring,
Something slightly troubling,
Something, at least, not transcendent.

Jeremy Cronin, 'Poem for Mandela', *Even the Dead* (1997)

Chronology

1846–7	Frontier 'War of the Axe' between British colonists in the eastern Cape, on the one hand, and the Xhosa and one branch of the Thembu people on the other.
1857	Cattle Killing movement in Transkei, led by prophetess Nongqawuse, leads to famine among the Xhosa people.
1877–8	Last Frontier War, in which migrant Thembu people support their neighbours, the Xhosa, and Transkei-based abaThembu support the British.
1894	Mohandas Gandhi founds Natal Indian Congress in Durban.
1899–1902	Anglo-Boer War.
1906	Bambata Zulu rebellion, sparked by refusal to pay poll-tax.
1910	Union of South Africa.
1912	Formation of South African Native National Congress (from 1923, the ANC).
1913	Native Land Act: 87 per cent of South Africa's land officially allocated to white people.
1918	End of World War I. 18 July: Nelson Mandela born in Mvezo, Transkei.
1920	Black miners' strike quashed. Mandela moves with his mother and sisters to Qunu following his headman father's dismissal by a white magistrate.

1923	South African Indian Congress formed.
1925	Mandela starts school and is given European name by teacher Miss Mdingane.
1926	Balfour Declaration.
1927	Legislation against interracial sexual relations. Following his father's death, Mandela goes to live with guardian, Chief Jongintaba.
1931	December: first pass-burning demonstrations.
1933	Coalition of Afrikaner parties under Hertzog and Smuts (collapses in 1939 with country's decision to go to war).
1934	Mandela circumcised along with his cousin Justice.
1935	Mandela enrols at Clarkebury Institute mission school.
1936	Native Land and Trust Act fixes 1913 land distribution in perpetuity. Africans lose Cape voting rights.
1937	Mandela attends Healdtown school.
1939	World War II begins. Mandela enrols at Fort Hare University to train as a civil servant.
1940	Hertzog and Malan launch reformed National Party. Mandela leaves Fort Hare without completing his degree after association with SRC strike.
1941	Mandela and Justice flee arranged marriages by running away to Johannesburg. Through businessman Walter Sisulu, Mandela finds a position as clerk with legal firm of Witken, Sidelsky and Eidelman, to complete a degree by correspondence, graduating in 1942.
1942	Mandela joins ANC.
1943	Enrols for LLB degree at Johannesburg's Witwatersrand University. August: successful Alexandra bus boycott. Formation and (in 1944) launch of ANC Youth League with Sisulu (treasurer), Oliver Tambo (secretary), and Mandela as executive member.

1944	Marries first wife Evelyn Mase. Completes legal articles and begins full-time study.
1945	Son Madiba Thembekile (Thembi) born.
1946	African mine workers' strike.
1947	Mandela elected to Transvaal provincial ANC executive and opposes SACP-SAIC-ANC 'Votes for All' campaign.
1948	Afrikaner Nationalist Party under Daniel Malan wins power with the explicit agenda of bringing racial segregation (apartheid) into law. First daughter Makaziwe born, who dies at 9 months.
1949	December: ANCYL gains control of ANC executive.
1950	Raft of new Acts—Population Registration, Group Areas, Suppression of Communism—hammers the white sepulchre of apartheid into place. ANCYL permits new multiracial policy. Mandela joins ANC national executive. 26 June: helps organize ANC-SAIC 'Day of Mourning'. September: elected ANCYL president. Second son, Makgatho, born.
1952	ANC-SAIC Defiance Campaign. Mandela placed under banning order. Passes attorney's professional examinations and opens legal office at Chancellor House, Johannesburg, with Tambo. Elected president of Transvaal Provincial ANC, then ANC deputy president. Albert Luthuli elected ANC president.
1953	Bantu Education Act. Mandela resigns from ANC to accommodate banning order.
1954	Sophiatown evictions. Daughter Pumla Makaziwe (Maki) born.
1955	26 June: Congress of the People at Kliptown, Johannesburg. Freedom Charter (foundation of future South African constitution) adopted. ANC's Bantu Education boycott fails.

1956	9 August: Women's March on Pretoria to protest against pass laws. Bus boycotts across Johannesburg. 6 December: 156 men and women representing ANC, SAIC, Coloured People's Congress, and Congress of Democrats arrested and charged with high treason. Treason Trial begins (–1961).
1957	Marriage to Evelyn breaks down.
1958	Mandela marries second wife, Nomzamo Winifred Madizikela (Winnie), a social worker.
1959	Pan-African Congress splits from ANC. International Anti-Apartheid Movement launched. Daughter Zenani born.
1960	21 March: Sharpeville massacre of sixty-nine black protestors under police fire. State of emergency declared: 20,000 arrested, 2,000 detained without trial. ANC and PAC banned. Daughter Zindziswa born.
1961	March: Treason Trial: accused found not guilty. Mandela disappears underground. South Africa, declared a republic, leaves the Commonwealth. December: launch of Umkhonto we Sizwe.
1962	Mandela travels in Africa and Europe: receives military training, meets leading activists and politicians. 5 August: he is captured in Kwazulu-Natal Midlands and sentenced to five years' imprisonment.
1963	90-Day Detention Act. Mandela sent to Robben Island. Recalled after Liliesleaf Farm raid, Rivonia. Charged with sabotage and planning an armed invasion. Rivonia Trial begins.
1964	20 April: Mandela delivers statement from dock. 12 June: eight Rivonia Trialists sentenced to life imprisonment.
1968	Steve Biko forms South African Students' Organization. Mandela's mother dies.
1969	May: Winnie Mandela detained under Terrorism Act for 491 days. July: Thembi dies in a car crash. Mandela not permitted to attend his funeral.

1974/5	Fall of Salazar's Portugal leads to independence of Angola and Mozambique.
	Mandela writes secret autobiography.
1976	Internal Security Act.
	South African invasion of Angola.
	16 June: Soweto students' uprising against Bantu Education leaves 618 dead, 1,500 wounded, over 13,000 arrested.
	Mandela refuses offer of conditional reduction of sentence.
1977	17 May: Winnie Mandela placed under banning order in Brandfort.
	12 September: Biko killed in detention and BC organizations banned.
1979	Mandela awarded Nehru Prize for International Understanding in absentia.
1980	Launch of worldwide Anti-Apartheid Movement (AAM) Release Mandela campaign.
	1 June: ANC Special Operations bombs SASOL oil refinery.
1982	Mandela and four other Rivonia prisoners moved to Pollsmoor Prison.
1983	Formation of UDF, embracing non-banned anti-apartheid organizations.
1984	Nationwide resistance to new constitution enshrining population segregation. Nkomati Accord between South Africa and Mozambique. Bishop Desmond Tutu awarded Nobel Peace Prize.
1985	31 January: P. W. Botha offers Mandela conditional freedom.
	11 February: Mandela responds with Soweto speech read by daughter Zindzi: a prisoner, like an unfree people, 'cannot give undertakings on violence'.
	Congress of South African Trade Unions formed.
	Resistance to apartheid builds across a broad front.
	20 July: state of emergency.
	December: Mandela has prostate operation. His first meeting with Minister of Justice Kobie Coetzee.

1986	Mandela meets Commonwealth Eminent Persons Group. 12 June: state of emergency renewed.
1987	November: first Rivonia prisoner Govan Mbeki released, due to ill health.
1988	February: UDF banned. March: South African defeat at Cuito Cuanavale. July: Free Mandela Campaign organizes 70th birthday celebrations at Wembley Stadium, London. December: Mandela transferred to Victor Verster after tuberculosis treatment.
1989	F. W. de Klerk takes over from Botha as state president.
1990	11 February: Mandela walks free. April: 'talks about talks' between government and ANC. August: ANC renounces use of arms.
1991	Mandela elected ANC president. December: Convention for a Democratic South Africa.
1992	White referendum shows pro-reform majority. Formal separation from Winnie.
1993	Assassination of SACP leader, Chris Hani. September: creation of transition executive council. October: Mandela and de Klerk jointly receive Nobel Peace Prize. 18 November: adoption of new constitution.
1994	27–28 April: nineteen million South Africans participate in first democratic elections. 10 May: Mandela inaugurated as president.
1995	Mandela awarded Order of Merit by Queen Elizabeth II. November: Nigerian writer-activist Ken Saro-Wiwa executed despite Mandela's diplomacy.
1996	April: Truth and Reconciliation Commission, modelled on Chile's 1990 Comisión, chaired by Archbishop Tutu, begins two years of hearing testimonies from apartheid's victims. Divorce from Winnie.
1998	Mandela marries Graça Machel.

1999	South Africa has highest number per capita of people living with HIV/AIDS in the world (four to five million = 10 per cent of population).
	June: ANC wins second general election. Mandela hands over to Thabo Mbeki.
2000	Mandela formally retires from public life.
2002	Formally promotes HIV/AIDS awareness.
	July: diagnosed with prostate cancer but responds well to treatment.
2003	Presides over the creation of the Mandela Rhodes Foundation to bring history full circle and extend his legacy of radical reconciliation. Inaugural ceremony in Westminster Hall, London.
2004	Further retreat from public life, epitomized in his favourite phrase: 'Don't call me, I'll call you'. Continues to show strong interest in his three legacy organizations: the Nelson Mandela Foundation, the Nelson Mandela Children's Fund, and the Mandela Rhodes Foundation.
2005	Announces son Makgatho's death from AIDS.
2006	Awarded Amnesty's Ambassador of Conscience award.
2007	Statue of Mandela unveiled in Westminster Square, London. Mandela inaugurates the Council of Elders.
2008	Mandela's 90th birthday celebrated with concerts in South Africa, Britain, and worldwide.
2013	5 December: Mandela dies at the age of 95 of a prolonged respiratory infection.
	15 December: State funeral held in Mandela's hometown of Qunu in the eastern Cape, South Africa.
2018	2 April: Death of Winnie Mandela.
2021	11 November: Death of F. W. de Klerk
	26 December: Death of Archbishop Desmond Tutu, hailed at his funeral by President Cyril Ramaphosa as the last of the great moral giants to preside over the birth of democratic South Africa.

Further reading

Chapter 1: Mandela: Story and symbol

On Mandela's life, useful biographies include:

Colin Bundy, *Nelson Mandela*, Jacana pocket series (Jacana, 2015).

Tom Lodge, *Mandela: A Critical Life* (Oxford University Press, 2006).

Fatima Meer, *Higher than Hope: The Authorized Biography of Nelson Mandela* (Hamish Hamilton, 1990 [1988]).

Anthony Sampson, *Mandela: The Authorized Biography* (Harper Collins, 2000).

On governing symbols:

Rita Barnard (ed.), *The Cambridge Companion to Nelson Mandela* (Cambridge University Press, 2014). Essays cited above include Bonner, Munro, Schalkwyk, Roux.

Elleke Boehmer, 'Postcolonial Terrorist: The Example of Nelson Mandela', *Parallax* 11 (2006): 46–55.

Elleke Boehmer, 'Madiba Magic: Nelson Mandela's Charisma', in *Political Leadership, Nations and Charisma*, ed. Margit Wunsch and Vivian Ibrahim (Routledge, 2012), pp. 161–70.

Nadine Gordimer, *Living in Hope and History* (Bloomsbury, 1990).

Isabel Hofmeyr, *The Portable Bunyan: A Transnational History of The Pilgrim's Progress* (Princeton University Press, 2004).

Martin Kalungu-Banda, *Leading like Madiba* (Double Storey, 2006).

Xolela Mangcu (ed.), *The Meaning of Mandela* (HCRC, 2006).

The complexities of life narrative:

James Clifford, 'Ethnobiographical Prospects', in *Studies in Biography*, ed. D. Aaron (Harvard University Press, 1978).

Liz Stanley, *The Autobiographical I* (Manchester University Press, 1992).

Cultural representation in Mandela's South Africa:

Annie E. Coombs, *History After Apartheid: Visual Culture and Public Memory in a Democratic South Africa* (University of the Witwatersrand Press, 2004).

Leon de Kock, Louise Bethlehem, and Sonja Laden (eds), *South Africa in the Global Imaginary* (UNISA Press, 2004).

Layered postcolonial modernity:

David Attwell, *Rewriting Modernity: Studies in Black South African Literary History* (University of Kwazulu-Natal Press, 2005).

Dipesh Chakrabarty, *Provincializing Europe: Postcolonial Thought and Historical Difference* (Princeton University Press, 2000).

Decolonial studies:

Gurminder K. Bhambra, Dalia Gebrial, and Kerem Nişancıoğlu (eds), *Decolonising the University* (Pluto Press, 2018).

Achille Mbembe, *Out of the Dark Night: Essays on Decolonization* (Columbia University Press, 2021).

Danai Mupotsa, *Feeling and Ugly* (Impepho, 2018).

Sabelo J. Ndlovu-Gatsheni, *The Decolonial Mandela: Peace, Justice and the Politics of Life* (Berghahn Books, 2016).

Frank B. Wilderson III, *Afropessimism* (Liveright, 2020).

Mandela's idioms:

Jennifer Cryws-Williams, *In the Words of Nelson Mandela* (Penguin, 1997).

Chapter 2: Scripting a life: The early years

On the iconography of national leaders:

Elleke Boehmer, *Stories of Women: Gender and Narrative in the Postcolonial Nation* (Manchester University Press, 2005).

Geoffrey Cubitt and Allen Warren (eds), *Heroic Reputations and Exemplary Lives* (Manchester University Press, 2000).

Philip Holden, *Autobiography and Decolonization* (Wisconsin University Press, 2006).

Colonial race pathologies:

W. E. B. Du Bois, *The Souls of Black Folk* (Barnes and Noble, 2003).

Frantz Fanon, *Black Skin, White Masks*, tr. Charles Lam Markmann (Pluto, 1986 [1952]).

Sizwe Mpofu-Walsh, *The New Apartheid* (Tafelberg, 2021).

Mandela—autobiographies/related memoirs:

Ahmed Kathrada, *Memoirs* (Zebra, 2004).

Nelson Mandela, *Long Walk to Freedom* (Little, Brown, 1994).

Frieda Bokwe Matthews, *Remembrances* (Mayibuye Books, 1995).

Elinor Sisulu, *Walter and Albertina Sisulu: In Our Lifetime* (Abacus, 2003).

Gillian Slovo, *Every Secret Thing: My Family, My Country* (Little, Brown, 1997).

Further biographies:

Mary Benson, *Nelson Mandela*, revised edn (Penguin, 1989).

Luli Callinicos, *Oliver Tambo: Beyond the Engeli Mountains* (David Philip, 2004).

Jean Guiloineau, *The Early Life of Rolihlahla Madiba Nelson Mandela*, tr. Joseph Rowe (North Atlantic Books, 2002).

Peter Limb, *Nelson Mandela: A Biography* (Greenwood Press, 2008).

Mac Maharaj (ed.), *Mandela: The Authorized Portrait* (PQ Blackwell, 2006).

Michael Meredith, *Nelson Mandela: A Biography* (Hamish Hamilton, 1997).

David James Smith, *Young Mandela* (Weidenfeld & Nicolson, 2010).

Mandela's own words:

Kader Asmal, David Chidester, and Wilmot James (eds), *In His Own Words: From Freedom to the Future* (Abacus, 2004).

Ruth First (ed.), *No Easy Walk to Freedom* (Heinemann, 1965).

International Defence and Aid Fund (ed.), *The Struggle Is My Life* (IDAF, 1978).

Nelson Mandela, *The Prison Letters of Nelson Mandela*, ed. Sahm Venter (W. W. Norton and Company, 2018).

Ato Quayson (ed.), *No Easy Walk to Freedom* (Penguin, 2002).

Chapter 3: Growth of a national icon: Later years

On apartheid and post-apartheid:

James Barber, *Mandela's World: The International Dimension* (James Currey, 1994).

William M. Gumede, *Thabo Mbeki and the Battle for the Soul of the ANC* (Zebra, 2005).

Robert Harvey, *The Fall of Apartheid* (Macmillan, 2001).

Paul S. Landau, 'The ANC, MK, and "The Turn to Violence" (1960–1962)', *South African Historical Journal* 64(3) (2012): 538–63.

Tom Lodge, *Politics in South Africa from Mandela to Mbeki* (James Currey, 2003).

Francis Meli, *South Africa Belongs to Us: A History of the ANC* (Zimbabwe Publishing House, 1988).

Brenna Munro, *South Africa and the Dream of Love to Come* (University of Minnesota Press, 2012).

Sarah Nuttall, *Entanglement: Literary and Cultural Reflections on Post-Apartheid* (Wits University Press, 2009).

Thula Simpson, *Umkhonto We Sizwe: The ANC's Armed Struggle* (Penguin Random House, 2016).

Thula Simpson, *History of South Africa: from 1902 to the Present* (Hurst, 2021).

Allister Sparks, *Tomorrow is Another Country* (Heinemann, 1995).

Winnie Mandela:

Anné Mariè Du Preez Bezdrob, *Winnie Mandela: A Life* (Zebra, 2003).

Emma Gilbey, *The Lady: The Life and Times of Winnie Mandela* (Vintage, 1994).

Sisonke Msimang, *The Resurrection of Winnie Mandela* (Jonathan Ball, 2018).

Njabulo Ndebele, *The Cry of Winnie Mandela: Novel* (David Philip, 2003).

Mandela's political analysis:

Nelson Mandela, '"Clear the Obstacles and Confront the Enemy", and "Whither the Black Consciousness Movement?"', in *Reflections in Prison*, ed. Mac Maharaj (Zebra, 2001).

Nelson Mandela, 'National Liberation', unpublished essay, quoted in Anthony Sampson's *Mandela*.

Chapter 4: Influences and interactions

On African nationalism in transnational context:

Colin Bundy and William Beinart, *Reassessing Mandela*, Southern African Studies (Jacana Media, 2020). Essays cited above include Hassim and Mangcu.

Paul Gilroy, *The Black Atlantic: Modernity and Double Consciousness* (Verso, 1993).

Walter Goebel and Saskia Schabio (eds), *Beyond the Black Atlantic* (Routledge, 2006).

Sheridan Johns and R. Hunt Davis, Jr, *Mandela, Tambo, and the African National Congress: The Struggle against Apartheid 1948–1990* (Oxford University Press, 1991).

George Padmore, *Pan-Africanism or Communism?* (Dennis Dobson, 1956).

Cross-border collaboration:

Elleke Boehmer, *Empire, the National, and the Postcolonial, 1880–1920* (Oxford University Press, 2002).

Leela Gandhi, *Affective Communities* (Duke University Press, 2006).

Robert Young, *Postcolonialism* (Blackwell, 2001).

Gandhi in South Africa:

Surendra Bhana, *Gandhi's Legacy: The Natal Indian Congress 1894–1994* (University of Natal Press, 1997).

Judith M. Brown and Martin Prozesky (eds), *Gandhi and South Africa* (University of Natal Press, 1996).

M. K. Gandhi, *An Autobiography; or The Story of My Experiments with Truth* (Navajivan Publishing House, 1958 [1927]).

Ramachandra Guha, 'When Eleven Young Women of Bengal Took on Gandhi', *The Telegraph* (7 January 2017).

Ramachandra Guha, *Gandhi: The Years That Changed the World, 1914–1948* (Allen Lane, 2018).

Eric Itzkin, *Gandhi's Johannesburg* (University of Witwatersrand Press, 2001).

Nelson Mandela, 'Gandhi the Prisoner', in *Mahatma Gandhi: 125 Years*, ed. B. R. Nanda (Indian Council for Race Relations, 1995).

Nelson Mandela, 'The Sacred Warrior—Nelson Mandela on Gandhi', *Time* (3 January 2000): www.sa-venues.com/nelson_mandela.htm

Nehru:

Jawaharlal Nehru, *An Autobiography*, revised edn (The Bodley Head, 1942).

Jawaharlal Nehru, *The Unity of India: Collected Writings 1937–1940* (John Day, 1942).

Jawaharlal Nehru, *The Discovery of India* (Oxford University Press, 2002).

Fanon:

Anthony Clayton, *The Wars of French Decolonization* (Longman, 1994).

Frantz Fanon, *The Wretched of the Earth*, tr. Constance Farrington (Penguin, 1986 [1961]).

Frantz Fanon, *Studies in a Dying Colonialism*, tr. Haakon Chevalier (Earthscan Press, 1989).

Frantz Fanon, *Alienation and Freedom*, ed. Jean Khalfa and Robert Young, tr. Steve Corcoran (Bloomsbury Academic, 2018).

Biko:

Steve Biko, *I Write What I Like* (Heinemann, 1978).

Nigel Gibson, 'Upright and Free: Fanon in South Africa, from Biko to the Shackdwellers' Movement (Abahlali baseMjondolo)', *Social Identities* 14(6) (2008): 683–715.

Xolela Mangcu, *Biko: A Life* (NB Publishers, 2014 [2012]).

Donald Woods, *Biko* (Paddington Press, 1978).

Chapter 5: Sophiatown sophisticate

On Africa and modernity:

John Comaroff and Jean Comaroff, *Of Revelation and Revolution* (University of Chicago Press, 1991).

J.-G. Deutsch et al. (eds), *African Modernities: Entangled Meanings in Current Debate* (James Currey, 2002).

The Sophiatown phenomenon:

Michael Chapman (ed.), *The Drum Decade: Stories from the 1950s*, 2nd edn (University of Natal Press, 2001).

David Coplan, *In Township Tonight!* (Ravan Press, 1985).

Bloke Modisane, *Blame Me on History* (Thames and Hudson, 1963).

Marlene van Niekerk, *Triomf*, tr. Leon de Kock (Little, Brown, 1999 [1994]).

Rob Nixon, *Homelands, Harlem, and Hollywood* (Routledge, 1994).

Lewis Nkosi, *Home and Exile* (Longman, 1965).

Anthony Sampson, *Drum: The Making of a Magazine*, 3rd edn (Jonathan Ball, 2005).

Derreck Thema, *Kortboy: A Sophiatown Legend* (Kwela Books, 1999).

Fictional/autobiographical reflections on Mandela:

Achmat Dangor, *Bitter Fruit* (Atlantic Books, 2003).

Ellen Kuzwayo, *Call Me Woman* (The Women's Press, 1985).

Winnie Mandela (and others), *Part of My Soul Went with Him* (Norton, 1985).

Lewis Nkosi, *Mandela's Ego* (Umuzi, 2006).

Poetry about Mandela:

Richard Bartlett (ed.), *Halala Madiba: Nelson Mandela in Poetry* (Aflame Books, 2006).

Jeremy Cronin, *Even the Dead* (Mayibuye Books, 1997).

Jeff Opland, *The Dassie and the Hunter* [about Thembu praise-poet David Manisi] (University of KZN Press, 2005).

Wole Soyinka, *Mandela's Earth* (André Deutsch, 1988).

Chapter 6: Masculine performer

Gender and nationalism:

Dorothy Driver, '*Drum Magazine* 1951–9 and Gender', in *Text, Theory, Space*, ed. Sarah Nuttall et al. (Routledge, 1993).

Ashis Nandy, *The Intimate Enemy* (Oxford University Press, 1983).

Jonny Steinberg, *Winnie and Nelson: Portrait of a Marriage* (Penguin Random House, 2023).

Rajeswari Sunder Rajan, *Real and Imagined Women* (Routledge, 1993).

Bodies under empire:

E. M. Collingham, *Imperial Bodies* (Polity, 2001).

Achille Mbembe, *Necropolitics* (Duke University Press, 2019).

Ann Laura Stoler, *Carnal Knowledge and Imperial Power* (University of California Press, 2002).

Mandela's self-representation:

J. M. Coetzee, 'The 1995 World Cup', in *Stranger Shores* (Secker, 2001).

Jacques Derrida and Mustafa Tlili (eds), *For Nelson Mandela*, tr. Franklin Philip et al. (Seaver Books, 1987 [1986]).

Zelda La Grange, *Good Morning, Mr Mandela* (Allen Lane, 2014).

John Kane, *The Politics of Moral Capital* (Cambridge University Press, 2001).

Philippe-Joseph Salazar, *An African Athens: Rhetoric and the Shaping of Democracy in South Africa* (Lawrence Erlbaum, 2002).

Chapter 7: Spectres in the prison garden

On embodying freedom and the future:

Hélène Cixous, *Manna for the Mandelstams for the Mandelas*, tr. Catherine McGillivray (Minnesota University Press, 1994).

Isidore Diala, 'Interrogating Mythology: The Mandela Myth and Black Empowerment', *Novel: A Forum on Fiction* 38(1) (2004): 41–56.

Robben Island:

The Robben Island General Recreational Committee Archive 1966–91, UWC-Robben Island Mayibuye Archives, MCH 64: 50–82.

Neville Alexander, *Robben Island Dossier 1964–74* (University of Cape Town Press, 1994).

Fran Lisa Buntman, *Robben Island and Prisoner Resistance to Apartheid* (Cambridge University Press, 2003).

Eddie Daniels, *There and Back: Robben Island 1964–1979*, 3rd edn (CTP Books, 2002).

Athol Fugard, John Kani, and Winston Ntshona, 'The Island', in *The Township Plays*, ed. Dennis Walder (Oxford University Press, 1993).

James Gregory, *Goodbye Bafana: Nelson Mandela, My Prisoner, My Friend* (Headline, 1995).

Mac Maharaj, *Reflections in Prison* (Zebra, 2001).

Spectrality:

Jacques Derrida, *Spectres of Marx*, tr. Peggy Kamuf (Routledge, 1994).

Jacques Derrida, 'Il faut toujours parler de L'Afrique du Sud au futur anterieur', *Newton Zebra* 11 (1998): 22–7.

Gardening as survival:

J. M. Coetzee, *Life and Times of Michael K* (Secker, 1983).

Verne Harris (ed.), *A Prisoner in the Garden: Opening Nelson Mandela's Prison Archive* (Nelson Mandela Foundation, 2004).

Bessie Head, *A Question of Power* (Heinemann, 1973).

Spatial construction:

Rita Barnard, *Apartheid and Beyond: South African Writers and the Politics of Place* (Oxford University Press, 2006).

Antoinette Burton, *Dwelling in the Archive: Women Writing Home* (Oxford University Press, 2003).

Patrick Bond, *Elite Transition: From Apartheid to Neo-liberalism in South Africa* (Pluto, 2000).

Hein Marais, *South Africa, Limits to Change*, 2nd edn (Zed Books, 2001).

Nation, self, other:

Kwame Anthony Appiah, *Cosmopolitanism* (Allen Lane, 2006).

Jacques Derrida and Anne Dufourmantelle, *Of Hospitality*, tr. Rachel Bowlby (Stanford University Press, 2000).

Simon Gikandi, 'Race and the Idea of the Aesthetic', *Michigan Quarterly Review* 40(2) (Spring 2001): 318–50.

Ghassan Hage, *Against Paranoid Nationalism* (Pluto, 2003).

Hans Ulrich Obrist, Gabriela Rangel, and Asad Raza (curators), *Lydia Cabrera and Édouard Glissant: Trembling Thinking*, The Americas Society (9 October 2018–12 January 2019).

Mandela for children:

Madiba Magic: *Nelson Mandela's Favourite Stories* (Tafelberg, 2002).

Mandela and memory:

Nelson Mandela and Mandla Langa, *Dare Not Linger*: *The Presidential Years* (Canongate, 2017).

Vimla Naidoo and Sahm Venter (eds), *I Remember Nelson Mandela* (Jacana, 2018).

Sarah Nuttall and Achille Mbembe, 'Mandela's Mortality', *The Cambridge Companion to Nelson Mandela*, ed. Rita Barnard (Cambridge University Press, 2014), pp. 267–90.

Koleka Putuma, '1994: A Love Poem', *Collective Amnesia* (uHlanga, 2017).

Hedley Twidle, *Firepool* (Kwela, 2017).

Index

For the benefit of digital users, indexed terms that span two pages
(e.g., 52–53) may, on occasion, appear on only one of those pages.

B

N

Index